Chakra Care

DO-IT-YOURSELF ENERGY HEALING FOR A
MORE JOYFUL, LOVING, FRUITFUL LIFE

Nancy Hausauer

Copyright © 2014 by Nancy Hausauer.

All rights reserved. No part of this publication may be reproduced, distributed or transmitted in any form or by any means, including photocopying, recording, or other electronic or mechanical methods, without the prior written permission of the author, except in the case of brief quotations embodied in critical reviews and certain other noncommercial uses permitted by copyright law. For permission requests, write to the author at the address below.

Nancy Hausauer
706 Sixth Avenue
Tacoma, WA 98405

Disclaimer: The author is not a medical doctor or mental health professional and is not providing medical or psychiatric counsel. This book is not intended to be a substitute for medical or psychiatric advice or care. For any physical or mental health concerns, seek the advice of a qualified doctor or mental health professional.

Cover design by Scott Bailey
Book layout ©2013 BookDesignTemplates.com

ISBN 978-1500716493

Contents

A Welcome To The World Of Energy Healing	1
What Is Energy?	3
I Have An Energy Body? Really? (What's That?)	5
What Are Chakras?	9
Why Do My Chakras Matter?	15
How Can I Tell If My Chakra System Is Healthy?	19
Answering A Few Common Questions About Chakra Imbalances	23
What Is Energy Healing? And Can I Really Do It?	27
How Do I Turn Simple Activities Into Chakra-Balancing Powerhouses?	31
First Chakra: Anchoring Yourself	35
Second Chakra: Getting in the Flow	49
Third Chakra: Coming From Your Place of Power	63
Fourth Chakra: Heart Wisdom	77
Fifth Chakra: Who Are You, Really?	91
Sixth Chakra: The Extraordinary Eye	105
Seventh Chakra: The Crowning Glory	119
Your Seven Chakras: A Holistic System	133

Three Techniques For Balancing Your Chakra System As A Whole	137
Some Final Thoughts	143
Appendices	
How To Ground	*145*
How To Center	*147*
How To Belly Breathe	*149*
How To Use Essential Oils	*153*
How To Use Affirmations	*157*
Glossary	159
Further Resources	161
Image Credits	162

Introduction

A Welcome To The World Of Energy Healing

Welcome to an exciting new way to look at your body and your life!

I've been studying and working with the chakras for almost 30 years. I find them infinitely fascinating, and I continue to learn more about them all the time.

But you don't have to study for 30 years to start working with your chakras! You can start using them as a tool for deeper health, harmony and happiness—today.

As an energy healer for 20 years and a writer for many more years than that, I'm passionate about helping other folks—people just like you—learn to work with their own energy (also called life force, bio-energy, chi, and many other names).

So I'm thrilled that you're interested in chakras. They're an important part of our "energy anatomy," and an important part of energy healing. (Don't worry, I'll explain all these concepts in the coming chapters.)

You may have heard of energy healing, and thought that it was something esoteric that you could never do. But absolutely without a doubt you can learn to do energy healing for your own chakras, allowing you to get to a deeper level of health and fulfillment in your life.

You don't have to have a special, rare gift or have years of training in obscure and complicated mysteries to work with your chakras. And you don't have to convert to any particular religious beliefs. Chakras, while they come from the Hindu wisdom tradition, transcend any particular religion.

There are an endless number of practical, down-to-earth things you can easily do to keep your chakras balanced, healthy and radiant. With a little knowledge and the almost magical power of intention, you <u>can</u> make a positive difference in your chakras and the other aspects of your energy, keeping them more balanced, flowing, harmonious and radiant.

Taking care of your energy will help you live a more healthy, joyful, loving and fruitful life. People will even be able to see it on your face. Your eyes will sparkle, you'll have a subtle glow to your skin, and you'll look more alive. You might find that after you've been working with your chakras for a while, people start telling you that you look great or asking if you've just come back from vacation!

I'm excited for you, as you begin this journey into the world of energy.

First, I'll give you a little bit of theory, to provide you with a basic orientation and background. Then we'll start getting into the specific chakras and how to work with them.

Are you ready? Then let's begin!

CHAPTER 1

What Is Energy?

Before we dive into the subject of chakras and learn how to work with them, there are a few basic concepts you'll need to understand.

The first one is "energy." I talk a lot about it—in fact this whole book is really about "energy" and "energy healing."

So what is energy? I'm obviously not talking about the kind of energy that runs your car or heats your house. And I'm not just taking about vitality, pep and "get-up-and-go," although physical vitality is one sign that your energy is healthy.

When I talk about energy, I mean life force, or even more generally, "being force." You might have heard it called prana, chi, ki, qi, spirit or bio-energy. It's the power that is the basis and animating force for our world and everything in it.

So energy, as I use the term in this book, is what gives us both being and life. It's the part of us that scientists, when they are describing our bodies and how they work, can't explain—where our consciousness, aliveness and very being come from.

From the smallest thing in the universe to the largest, energy generates us, constitutes us, animates us, surrounds us, permeates us, sustains us and connects us to all other things. As science asserts, everything is energy. And though it can be invisible, like the air you breathe, it's just as real.

You may think that this somewhat intangible "energy" is something that only a few gifted people can perceive and understand—but that's not the case. You constantly experience energy and interact with it. For example:

- When you walk into someone's home and instantly do or don't like the way it feels
- When you're in a forest, and have a feeling of deep peace and renewal
- When you put your arm around a troubled friend, and she feels better
- When you have a hunch or an intuition about something
- When you speak up and bring calm and reason back to a group that has become angry and irrational
- When you liven up a dull party
- When you clean your house
- When you talk or interact with someone
- When you breathe
- When you're alive!

Energy is everywhere and everything, as common—and as miraculous—as the air we breathe, the light of the sun and stars, the love of family and friends. And you (yes, you!) can influence it in purposeful ways to make your life healthier, happier and more satisfying. Influencing energy in this purposeful, positive way is called energy healing. Later I'll show you just how easy it can be to do energy healing for yourself.

But first, let's talk about your particular, unique energy, the energy that makes you you—your personal energy body.

CHAPTER 2

I Have An Energy Body? Really? (What's That?)

The world (by which I mean the totality of everything that exists) has its own energy field. In addition, every individual being and thing in the world has its own individual energy field, which is contained within the larger, universal field. What I'm saying is that you, like everyone and everything else, have your own personal energy field, a distinct energy that surrounds you and permeates you.

Your field is both a part of the larger field and also in some ways separate from it. To give an analogy, the larger or universal field can be compared to the ocean and your personal energy field to a drop of water in that ocean. The drop—you—is part of the ocean and yet at the same time, in some circumstances, separate from it.

Another analogy for the simultaneously part-of/separate-from state of your personal energy field is an individual within a crowd of people. If you're standing in a crowd, the crowd has its own separate being. You, as an individual within that crowd, are part of the crowd, but you also have a separate identity. Your individual energy field is like that.

I will often refer to this individual or personal energy field as the energy body, or also as the energy system or human energy field.

Like energy in general, your energy body is very real, but for most people it's too subtle to see or touch (unless you count the physical body as part of the energy field, which I do, but that's a discussion for another book). Invisible though it is, your energy field has a huge impact on your physical health and on your life.

You might think that your physical body generates your energy field, but it's actually the other way around! Your energy body comes first, and generates your physical body as well as your thoughts and emotions.

This is a very important concept, because it means that the state of your energy body determines the state of your physical body, mind, emotions and life. If your energy is healthy, you're going to feel good. But if it's disturbed, you're going to feel consequent disturbances in your thoughts, emotions, or mood, and possibly even in your physical body and your life.

If your energy is "off," you might, for example, get a headache, feel anxious, have an up-set stomach, have a fight with a friend or just generally have a bad day. If your energy is disturbed over a long period of time, it can manifest as more serious illnesses or life problems.

The good news is that the opposite is true as well, and that there are many ways you can positively influence your own energy body so that your physical body thrives, your mind is clear and strong, your emotions are balanced and enriching, and your life is more joyful, satisfying and productive.

Your Energy Body's Anatomy

Just like your physical body, your energy body is orderly and has features and structures and what we might call "energy-organs." Some of the main features of your energy-anatomy are:

- The aura, also called the energy field or electromagnetic field, which surrounds your physical body like a cocoon of light.

- Meridians, which are energy pathways or channels in your body, like a circulatory system for energy. Acupuncture and acupressure work with the meridians.

- Chakras, which are energy centers and portals in your energy field.

While different individuals and cultures have conceived of or focused on different parts of the energy anatomy, these are some of the basics that most people today agree on. In the next chapter, I'll explain what chakras are.

CHAPTER 3

What Are Chakras?

Chakras are a vitally important part of your energy body. The chakras—there are seven main ones—are concentrated, especially active areas of energy within your energy field. They play a critical role in the health of your energy system, including your physical body.

You can learn a lot about yourself by exploring your chakras, and you can also work with the chakra system to improve your life and your health. For example, working with your chakras can help you:

- Overcome anxiety to feel more calm and secure
- Have more pleasure, fun and creativity in your life

- Develop your personal power, self-esteem and vitality
- Heal troubled relationships and form meaningful new relationships
- Speak your truth and create a life that truly expresses who you are
- Gain wisdom, clarity, intuition and perspective
- Develop a connection to something greater, find meaning in your life, experience more wonder and feel more inner peace.

The chakras are located along the midline of your physical body/energy body from the base of your spine to the top of your head. They can be visualized as spinning, cone-like shapes or vortices. The five middle chakras project horizontally into your energy field from both the front and the back of your body, while the first, at the base of your spine, projects downward and the seventh, at the top of your head, projects upward. The chakras are arrayed along the central channel of your energy body. Energy flows up and down this channel, linking and integrating all seven chakras and their various energies.

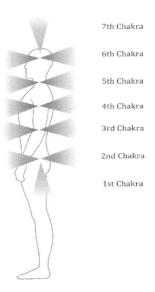

The chakras are an interface between your personal energy and the universal energy. Through them, energy flows into and out of you in a never-ending exchange with the larger, universal energy field. In this way, your chakras are a little like your lungs. Each exchanges invisible substances with the outside world – the chakras exchanging energy and the lungs exchanging air and carbon dioxide (although your lungs work in a rhythmic fashion, while the flow of energy through your chakras is constant).

The chakras are also a little like your digestive system. They receive, absorb and transmit life energies to your body-mind, similar to the way your digestive system receives and metabolizes food.

Your chakras interface with your physical body primarily through your endocrine glands and spine.

Each of the seven major chakras acts as a conduit for a particular form of energy, assimilating and distributing it to specific physical, mental, emotional and spiritual functions. Thus, each chakra corresponds to, nourishes and organizes the life energy for specific body areas, organs and facets of your being and your life, as summarized on the following page.

The Seven Chakras And Their Associations

Number	Common English Name	Location	Related Body Areas	Associated With
1	Root Chakra	Base of spine	Bones, tailbone, legs, feet, colon	Physical self, self-preservation, survival instincts, connection to our bodies and the earth, abundance, family of origin
2	Sacral Chakra	Lower abdomen	Sexual organs, bladder, kidneys, lower back, pelvis	Sexuality, emotions, pleasure, creativity, sensation, flow
3	Solar Plexus Chakra	Upper abdomen between naval & sternum	Digestive system, immune system, adrenal glands, muscles	Ego, will, metabolism, personal power, personal boundaries, personal identity, logical thought
4	Heart Chakra	Center of chest at heart level	Lungs, thymus, heart, respiratory & cardiac systems, arms, hands	Love, integration, self-love, compassion, healing, relationships, connection to nature, connection to universal love
5	Throat Chakra	Base of throat	Throat/neck, shoulders, mouth, ears, nose, sinuses, thyroid & parathyroid glands	Communication, self-expression, creativity, truth, authenticity, self-actualization
6	Brow Chakra/ Third Eye	Forehead, between & slightly above eyebrows	Eyes, pineal gland, hypothalamus, medulla plexus	Sight, both physical and intuitive/psychic; higher intellect; insight
7	Crown Chakra	Top of head	Upper skull, cerebral cortex, central nervous system, pituitary gland	Spiritual life and experience, deep self-knowledge, sense of oneness/unity, relationship with the Divine, pure consciousness, transcendence

The idea of chakras comes to us primarily from Hindu and Buddhist wisdom traditions, but similar concepts are noted in many other cultures as well.

While each of the chakras is interesting and valuable in its own right, it is as a system that they are most rightly viewed and powerfully worked with. Together, they encompass every aspect of a human life and taken as a whole are a tool for developing wholeness and balance and for fostering personal and spiritual growth. Each is critical, none can be ignored and none should be prized over another.

All in all, the chakra system is an elegant way of looking at the whole human being, one that helps us gain insight into ourselves; develop and integrate essential aspects of ourselves; move toward greater health, happiness and wholeness; and evolve toward our highest potential.

CHAPTER 4

Why Do My Chakras Matter?

Chakras are a critical part of your energy system, distantly comparable to both the lungs and the digestive system in your physical body. Just as you want your physical organs to be working well, you also want your energy-organs to be working well.

Your chakras, when healthy, are open, balanced, aligned, clear and radiant. Energy flows freely and in a balanced way in and out of each chakra and between the chakras as well, at a rate that is optimal for you at any particular moment.

However, it's common for one or more chakras to be partially blocked, imbalanced or out of harmony.

Blockages and other imbalances, whether they occur in the physical body or the energy body, aren't good. It goes without saying that a blocked artery, a blocked airway, clogged lungs or even a stuffy nose is going to cause you health problems.

Blockages in the flow of energy through your chakras will also cause you problems. The results will be less dire and less immediate than a blocked airway, but over time they're going to have a negative impact.

When Your Chakras Are Disturbed Or Imbalanced, **You** Become Disturbed Or Imbalanced

Chakra imbalances, disturbances or blockages can show up on any level of your being— physical, emotional, mental or spiritual. Your body, your life or both may be knocked out of balance.

Sound healing expert Jonathan Goldman gives a helpful analogy. He compares the body/energy body to a musical orchestra, where the individual players represent physical or energetic organs. If one "instrument" (such as a chakra) gets off tune or out of balance, the sound of the entire orchestra (the health of your entire physical and energetic body) is off, and pretty soon the other players (other parts of your physical or energetic system) start to veer off-tune, too. You want every instrument/physical organ/energy-organ to be working in harmony.

When one or more chakras are blocked, out of balance or otherwise less than completely healthy, there will be some aspect of your life, health, mind, or emotions that isn't functioning well.

For example, you may feel anxious, dull, listless, restless, frantic, depressed, low-energy, stressed, foggy, angry or sad for no reason. You may have a characteristic illness, or just a lot of illnesses. You may have chronic pain in your body. Your life may be chaotic, unsatisfying, seem like a soap opera, feel dry and repetitive, or seem like something important is missing. You may have difficulties with relationships or in your career, or may have a run of accidents or bad luck. Somewhere in your life, things will not be going smoothly.

Later chapters will provide much more detail about how to determine whether each individual chakra is healthy or unhealthy, in or out of balance.

When Your Chakras Are Healthy And Balanced, **You** Are Healthy And Balanced

Conversely, when your chakra system is healthy and running pretty smoothly, your life is likely to run pretty smoothly. A healthy chakra system won't necessarily make your life a bed of roses or immediately heal all your physical ailments, but you'll feel a basic sense of vitality, "glad-to-be-aliveness," peace with how things are for you at the moment and satisfaction with the direction they're heading. Your problems won't all instantly be solved (nor would you want them to be, since problems are opportunities for growth), but you'll have a sense that things are basically right with your life. You'll feel more centered, energized and in tune with yourself. It's a good feeling.

But it goes beyond that. When your chakras are healthy, balanced and radiant, it allows you greater personal and spiritual growth. It speeds up your process of personal evolution, helping you move more quickly beyond anxiety, jealousy and insecurity toward greater optimism, love, creativity and compassion. It helps you appreciate this beautiful life that we're given and contribute more to the world around you and the ones you love. In other words, it helps you grow, in this lifetime, toward being your highest self.

CHAPTER 5

How Can I Tell If My Chakra System Is Healthy?

So what constitutes a healthy chakra and a healthy chakra system? And how do you tell, since you can't take their temperature, hear them cough or see with your eyes whether they look pale and sickly or robust and thriving?

In a thriving chakra system:

- All of the chakras are open, so that energy can flow vertically up and down the central channel, reaching each chakra. Energy also flows horizontally, so that each chakra smoothly exchanges energy with the cosmos.
- None of the chakras is substantially more open or spinning significantly faster or slower than the others. None is significantly overactive or underactive in comparison to the rest.

- Each of the chakras is opened to the degree needed to support health and spiritual development. None of the seven chakras is open too wide or closed down too tight.
- The color of each chakra is clear, not muddy.
- Each chakra generally spins clockwise.
- Neither the upper chakras nor the lower chakras are over-emphasized.

But don't worry! If you're wondering how in the heck you're going to figure out whether your chakras are open or closed, spinning or not, clear or muddy—fortunately there are easy ways to tell. We'll leave specific perceptions of the chakras to professional energy healers. For our purposes, you'll be able to get all the information you need by looking at your body and your life. That's because an imbalance in your chakra system will eventually manifest in your body, emotions, thoughts or life. In other words, it will show up clearly in the physical world at some point.

In the later chapters on each individual chakra we'll be getting down to details, but here's how someone's life might look if all seven chakras were functioning optimally:

- A relatively healthy physical body with good vitality (or at least healthy and viable enough to support her or his spiritual journey or life purpose—I once knew a profoundly disabled man whose body was a magnificent vehicle for his spiritual path)
- The practical side of life basically in order, however he or she defines that
- A basic sense of security and safety in the world
- In touch with his or her emotions without being overwhelmed by them
- An ability to experience joy

- A healthy sexuality
- A balance between work and play
- Some form of creative pursuits or play
- A basic sense of self-worth
- An ability to make things happen in the physical world
- Healthy personal boundaries
- Meaningful work, making a contribution to the larger community or world
- Absence of addictions
- Balanced, healthy relationships and a sense of emotional contentment
- An ability to feel compassion for others
- A connection to nature and/or community
- An ability to express his or her own truth and to listen as well as talk
- Clear thought processes
- Access to intuition and wisdom
- A personal sense of ethics
- Some form of spiritual life or sense of meaning and larger purpose in life.

Of course, this would be an ideal person, one who really had his or her act (and energy) together in mind, body and spirit. Not too many of us are at this ideal state, and that's fine. We're human beings, which is to say we're incomplete, all of us put here with things we need to learn and ways we need to grow in this lifetime.

CHAPTER 6

Answering A Few Common Questions About Chakra Imbalances

In the previous chapter, I mentioned that chakra imbalances and blockages are common. Here are answers to some questions that often arise about chakra imbalances or disturbances.

Are chakra imbalances common? Are they something I need to be worried about?

It's commonplace for one or more chakras to become blocked, imbalanced, or out of tune, as another way to put it. It's a normal thing, just part of being human.

Chakra imbalances are not something to be concerned and anxious about. Rather than seeing them as something to worry about, I view them as an opportunity to grow and develop. By becoming aware of where our chakras are out of balance or could be healthier and by working to clear, balance and strengthen them, we can make our lives healthier and happier. As I like to think of it, the seven chakras offer seven pathways to a more joyful, loving, fruitful life. I think that's something to celebrate rather than worry about.

If one or more of my chakras is out of balance or unhealthy, does that mean there's something wrong with me—a standard of perfection that I'm not measuring up to?

No. It's really important to remember that a chakra being out of balance or harmony is within the context of YOUR energetic system and YOUR personal evolution or growth. It is not an absolute. In other words, if I were to tell you that your 3rd chakra is overactive, I mean in relationship to your other chakras, not in relation to some absolute ideal of how a perfect third chakra ought to be.

And if one of your chakras is "needing development," or needing to be more active or opened wider, once again that is not in comparison to anything outside of you. Rather, it is usually a sign that YOUR energy system is ready and willing for a new step toward health and wholeness, ready to enter a new stage of evolution and growth, ready to take another step toward your own highest potential. That's good!

Does each of my chakras need to be opened the exact same amount, allowing energy to flow to the exact same degree?

No. While overall balance is important in the chakra system, there's no need to strive to have each chakra exactly the same. Differences in the chakras, in their openness and strength and so on, are normal and can even be desirable. It's part of what creates your personality, your uniqueness and the distinctive gifts you bring to the world.

What causes chakra imbalances?

Chakras can become imbalanced for many reasons. Just to name a few:

- Negative thoughts and emotions can block or distort the flow of energy in a chakra.
- Long periods of overwork can deplete a chakra.
- Overemphasis on a particular aspect of life (such as the material side of life) can result in an imbalance.
- Emotional trauma can cause a variety of disturbances in the chakras.
- A person's upbringing, environment or culture can lead to chakra imbalances.
- We can be born with a particular chakra imbalance, with part of our life's work being to restore it to harmony.
- Development in one chakra can create a need for readjustment in other chakras.
- A new insight, readiness for personal growth or life development (e.g. marriage, parenthood or old age) can cause a particular chakra to need to open more in response.

CHAPTER 7

What Is Energy Healing? And Can I Really Do It?

Before we launch into learning more about each of the seven chakras and how to influence them in positive ways, there's another concept you need to know. That's the concept of energy healing. Why? Because you're going to be doing simple energy healing for yourself in just a little while.

What Is Energy Healing?

Energy healing is any method of working with an individual's energy field, or an aspect of it such as the chakras, to influence it toward greater health, wholeness, balance and growth.

For most people, if they've even heard of energy healing, it seems like a pretty esoteric thing, something that they could never do.

But I want you to know that there are lots of different ways to do energy healing, and you CAN do some of them, with just the things you'll learn in this book.

Energy healing—also called energy work, energy medicine, spiritual healing and laying on of hands—recognizes and works with the more subtle aspects of an individual's nature—his or her energy. As you may recall, "energy" is life-force and being-force. It animates us and is the foundation and template for physical being. Though universal in nature, it takes a unique and beautiful form in each one of us.

Professional energy healers usually work directly with another person's energy, influencing it toward greater health and balance with their hands and also sometimes their voices, eyes and thoughts. Some energy healers work with their hands directly on the physical body, some work with their hands above the body, in the field, and many do both. However they do it, they are using energy to influence energy.

Sometimes they have trained for years to be energy healers, and sometimes it's a natural gift that expresses itself without training. Some kinds of energy healing that you may have heard of include Reiki, acupressure and acupuncture, and Healing Touch.

You Can Do Simple Energy Healing, Too

Though some people feel a special calling and make energy healing part or all of their life's work, everyone has the ability to do at least some energy healing—and most of us actually do it a lot already.

We are always influencing other people's energy. We can't help it —it just happens naturally. We influence the energy of others by what we say to them, how we look at them, how we touch them, our mood, our tone of voice, the food we give them, the environment we create, our feelings and thoughts about them and so on. In short, just about everything we are and do influences the energy of others.

Whenever you interact with people in a positive, loving manner, you're influencing their energy in a healing way, which is to say—you're doing energy healing. If you ever comfort a sad friend, soothe a fussy child or kiss a skinned knee to make it feel better, you're already doing simple, every-day energy healing.

In this book, I'm not going to teach you any specific energy healing techniques to work with other people. But I will show you many down-to-earth, almost ordinary ways to do energy healing for your own chakras.

You may be wondering, "If these techniques are so down-to-earth and ordinary, how are they going to work?"

Well, there's a "secret ingredient" to turbo-charge ordinary activities with energy-healing power.

And that ingredient is . . .

CHAPTER 8

How Do I Turn Simple Activities Into Chakra-Balancing Powerhouses?

Using The Power Of Intention To Activate The Exercises In This Book

As I was saying, in the chapters ahead you're going to find many specific activities and practices for working with the individual chakras, and some (though not all) of them sound pretty ordinary: work in your garden, go for a walk, spend time with kids or your dog. . . .

How is it that ordinary activities like these can "do" anything? How can they impact your energy-body, such as your chakras?

First, energy is actually pretty easy to influence! It's moving and changing all the time, with what we think, what we feel, what we do. So it's actually not a stretch to think that an ordinary activity like walking your dog could influence your energy. It does!

But you're also going to do something to turbo-charge these ordinary activities, adding a "secret ingredient" that multiplies their power and impact.

This "secret ingredient" is **intention**. You may have heard experts like Dr. Wayne Dyer talk about the "power of intention," and it's really true. Our thoughts have great power, and when we consciously focus them on a purpose or goal (in other words, when we create an intention), they can make amazing things happen.

How to Create An Intention

All of the techniques, methods, exercises and practices I share with you in this book are really only tools, only aids. It's the intention behind the techniques that's the most important thing.

So before doing any of the simple activities I suggest in the following chapters, set an intention. How do you do that? Easy.

Say you determine that your first chakra could use some balancing and support. From the list of activities that are beneficial for the first chakra, you decide that you are going to work in your garden.

Before gathering up your gardening gloves and shovel and snippers, say or write something such as "I am going to work in my garden with the intention of nourishing and balancing my first chakra and helping myself feel more calm, grounded and aware of the abundance I already have."

Then, go gardening! Enjoy yourself! You don't need to concentrate ferociously on your intention the whole time, but do occasionally take a moment to silently affirm it.

That's really all there is to it. Your intention will shift your energy and have a positive impact on your first chakra. And you will almost certainly come away from your afternoon feeling more calm, grounded and aware of the abundance you already have.

And that's how any intentionally done activity, no matter how humble or mundane, can be used to heal and support your chakras and start a transformational process in your life. Can you just "intend," without the activity? Yes, but it's a whole lot harder to do. The outward actions help to focus the power of your thoughts and bring them through into the physical world.

Now—on to the hands-on part of this book, where you actually get to work with your chakras.

CHAPTER 9

First Chakra: Anchoring Yourself

Get Beyond Anxiety To A Sense Of Peace And Security

The first chakra, also called the root chakra, is located at the base of the spine. Its keyword is "survival." Rather than projecting horizontally out from the body as the middle five chakras do, it projects downward, toward the earth.

The root chakra is very primal. It relates to the physical body, self-preservation, survival instincts, connection to the earth, family of origin, the ability to provide for oneself, and having a basic sense of safety, security and belonging in the world. It provides the necessary aspect of structure to a life.

When the first chakra is unbalanced, we feel like our feet are knocked out from under us, we're on edge, or we're "losing our grip." A healthy first chakra can help us relax, feel more calm, grounded and secure, and let go of nagging fears. It can help us feel that we truly belong in the universe, that we will have what we need to sustain physical life and that everything will turn out basically all right.

With these most basic of functions, the first chakra is the foundation for physical health and for the development of all the other chakras. When we feel deeply secure and have the practical side of life under control, we can turn our attention to more interesting things—hobbies, relationships, art, career, learning, volunteering, community betterment, spiritual development—the possibilities are endless. And that's a good feeling!

Its color is red, and it is related to the element of earth.

First Chakra At A Glance

Common English name	Root Chakra
Location	Base of spine
Associations	Physical self, self-preservation, survival instincts, connection to our bodies and the earth, abundance, relationships with family of origin
Related organs	Bones, tailbone, legs, feet, colon
Related sense	Smell
Related color	Red
Related element	Earth
Ideal level of functioning	Physical health and vitality, sense of abundance, sense of security and ease in the world, stable, orderly life, ability to manage stress well, general feeling that things will work out OK

Is Your First Chakra Healthy?

Someone with a healthy root chakra will usually have a basic sense of security and safety in the world. You will be well grounded and people will think of you as having "common sense." You will have a strong will to live.

The practical side of your life will usually function fairly smoothly. Bills get paid, meals happen on time, birthday cards get sent. You tend to be stable and well organized. Your life has structure.

You may or may not be wealthy, but you'll enjoy a sense of having (or being able to get) enough material resources to meet your needs. You are most likely very prudent financially, which may result in increasing abundance over time. However, you will not be flashy or extravagant.

You may enjoy traditions and be fairly conventional, at least in some respects. You may settle down in one place and stay there for a long time—at any rate, that's probably what you're most comfortable with. You like to put down roots. If you have a more nomadic lifestyle, you're likely to be very good at creating a sense of home wherever you land.

You probably have a comfortable home and enjoy a good, hearty meal. You may enjoy gardening, family gatherings and outdoor activities. You'll work hard, but have a good balance between work and the other aspects of your life.

Family will be important to you. If you're a parent, you'll make it a priority to create a stable, healthy home environment for your kids. If you're a pet-owner, you'll take good care of your animal companions. If your parents are alive, you're the kind of daughter or son who will stay in close contact, with regular visits or calls and good intentions to care for them as they age.

You will be fairly at ease with your own body, as well as your life in general. You are likely to have good vitality and be relatively healthy, especially your bones, feet, legs and colon.

Is Your First Chakra Out Of Balance?

If your first chakra is out of balance, you will have issues with groundedness, security, structure and stability—either too much or too little. You will be either too comfortable and settled in the world, lacking the fire to change and grow, the inspiration to create, the lightness to laugh and play—or you will be the opposite— anxious, unstable, flighty.

If your first chakra is weak or underactive, your will to live—your survival instinct—may be weak, or you might live in a constant state of anxiety and worry whose basis, though not necessarily clear on the surface, is a primal fear of not being able to survive. This deep-seated concern about safety and survival could show up either as excessive fear or as aggression and defensiveness. You may have a persistent feeling of not belonging anywhere, that the world is a cold and hostile place and that nobody "has your back." You might be prone to panic attacks.

If your first chakra is overactive, you may be ultra-conservative, complacent, highly status-conscious, set in your ways and completely satisfied with the status quo. Others may think of you as controlling. You may be overly identified with your "tribe" (e.g. your family, sports team, ethnic/cultural group or country) and may be all too eager to fight for them.

When the first chakra is out of balance, there are often issues with money. You might be "all about money," lacking in generosity or obsessed with acquiring wealth. You may have difficulty letting go of money and possessions. On the other end of the spectrum, you might be constantly scrambling to pay the rent. You might let go of money too freely, gambling, running up debt, giving money away or generally having difficulty managing your resources.

If your first chakra is chronically out of balance, you may have had a difficult childhood, including childhood trauma, abuse, extreme poverty or neglect.

If you have children, you may have difficulty settling into your role as a parent (underactive first chakra), or, on the other hand, you might be overly rigid (overactive first chakra). If your first chakra is underdeveloped or blocked, home may be chaotic, or you might move a lot, never really settling into a home or a community. On the other hand, if your first chakra is overactive, you may have the kind of home where everything must be just so, rules are set in stone, children are expected to obey no matter what, and your family is afraid to touch anything for fear of disturbing its rigid perfection.

If your first chakra is underactive or blocked, you might be ungrounded, and people may consider you flaky or unreliable. On the other end of the spectrum, if your first chakra is overactive or open too wide, you might be overly practical, plodding and lacking in dreams, vision, intuition and imagination. You might feel stuck in a rut but unable to see a way out of it.

With regard to your physical body, you might have problems with your bones, feet, legs, colon, elimination or weight. Stress and anxiety may take a toll on you. You might wish you had more physical vitality or a stronger constitution. You might worry a lot about your health or, on the other hand, be obsessed with diet and exercise.

Work With Your First Chakra If...

In summary, it would benefit you to clear, balance and support your first chakra if several or more of these statements apply to you:

- You feel like you're "losing your grip."
- You are often anxious or stressed and find it hard to relax.
- You worry a lot, have nagging fears or wake up in the middle of the night with gnawing anxiety.
- You have panic attacks.
- In general, you feel that the world is a hostile place and that things are probably not going to turn out OK.
- You would like better family relations.
- You would like more stability, order and structure in your life.
- You're not very good with the practical side of life.
- You feel stuck, in a rut or like you're just plodding along in life.
- You wish you had more "common sense."
- You never feel like you have enough money and you worry a lot about it.
- You have trouble managing money.
- Your parents or mate are gravely ill or have recently passed on.
- You were abused or neglected as a child or had other childhood traumas.
- You feel like childhood issues interfere with your ability to be a good parent.
- You'd like to have more physical vitality.
- You grew up in extreme poverty.
- Your country or region is extremely economically unstable.
- Your sense of smell is "off."
- You have nagging concerns about your health.

- You've had a lot of illnesses, accidents or surgeries.
- You have issues with your bones, feet, legs, colon or weight.
- You are often constipated.
- You have irritable bowel syndrome.
- You live in an area that is torn by revolution, war or natural disaster.
- You've recently been in a life-threatening situation, such as a car crash.
- You've recently been the victim of a crime.
- You've recently moved to a new home
- You've recently traveled a long ways, especially by air, and are having difficulty getting back to normal life.
- Your will to live is weak. Sometimes it feels like life is too much trouble.

How To Clear, Balance And Nurture Your First Chakra

Here are some pleasant, practical, "real-world" things you can do to support first chakra health and radiance. Once you see the pattern, I'm sure you'll be able to think of more. Remember, intention is the "secret ingredient."

Activities

- Take time every day, say five or ten minutes, to belly breathe. Belly breathing is deep, slow breathing all the way into the lower third of your lungs. Many people breathe quickly and shallowly. Make sure that your belly is rising when you breathe in, and falling when you breathe out. Slow your breathing down and enjoy the feeling of the air coming into and out of your lungs. (See Appendix 3 for more detailed instructions.)
- Walk. Get some good shoes, make a commitment to walk most days and then do it. If you have a chance, slip off your shoes and walk barefoot in the grass, dig your toes into the dirt or walk on the beach.
- Dance. Whether you're on a dance floor, playing with your children or all alone in your living room doesn't matter. Turn on some music and let yourself go, particularly using your feet, legs and pelvis.
- Get out in your garden and dig in the dirt. If you don't have a garden, plant something in a container.
- Compost your kitchen scraps and garden trimmings.
- Resolve to keep your thoughts more in the here and now.
- Learn to ground and center. (See Appendices 1 and 2.)

Physical Body

- Hold the acupressure point "Bubbling Spring" (Kidney 1), on the bottoms of your feet in the fleshy area about one third of the way between the base of your third toe and the end of your heel (approximately centered horizontally). Hold for one minute.
- If you have any nagging health concerns or if you're just overdue for a general check-up with your doctor, schedule an appointment now.
- Sit less. If you have a desk job, take regular breaks. Consider a standing desk.
- Take a stress management class.
- Do strength-and endurance-building exercises.
- Take good care of your feet. Invest in comfortable shoes; give yourself a pedicure or foot rub and see a foot doctor if you have any long-term issues.
- Get a good night's sleep. Make a point of going to bed and getting up at regular times.

Home

- Create healthy order and structure in your home, for example making a filing system for organizing your papers, putting up shelves or cleaning a messy closet.
- Take care of unfinished business, projects and tasks.
- If you have a good relationship with your family of origin, hang pictures of them. Display items that remind you of good times from your childhood.
- Clean and organize the garage or basement.
- If you have belongings scattered in various places, take steps to consolidate and "bring them home."
- Plant a tree.

- Revive traditions from your culture of origin.
- Balance your checkbook or otherwise get your finances in order.

Family, Friends and Community

- If your parents are alive and you have a decent relationship with them, call them up or make plans to visit them. If your grandparents are living, ask them to tell you stories from the old days.
- If you have children, plan a family night or outing that you'll all enjoy.
- If important structures and rituals of your family life such as regular bedtimes and mealtimes have slipped a bit, take steps to re-establish them.
- Learn more about your family tree.
- Reconnect with old friends.
- Put together a family picture album. If you have children, look at old albums together.
- If you have children, teach them a basic life skill (and repeat until they leave home or beyond!). If you yourself are missing a basic life skill (e.g. cooking), learn to do it.

Food

Eat regular meals. Plan a week's worth of healthy menus and go shopping so that you have everything you need to prepare them. Be sure to include at least one recipe from your childhood that brings back memories of happiness and contentment. Eat healthy food, especially root vegetables such as carrots, beets, yams or potatoes, and make sure you're getting enough protein and fiber in your diet.

Work and Career

- Tidy your workspace. Take care of your tools. File papers.
- Show up on time, every day.

- Return phone calls and get caught up on emails.
- Finish undone projects and tie up loose ends.
- What is your core function at your job? Re-evaluate it. How are you doing? How could you do it better? How could you reinvigorate it/renew your enthusiasm for it?
- Look for ways to make your primary income source more secure. Are there skills you need to learn, new technologies you need to master, people you need to become allies with, areas of your job in which you need to improve your performance or ways you can contribute more directly to the core function of your organization?
- If you're in a shaky or volatile industry, explore ways that you might switch to a more secure, stable field.
- If you have reason to think that you might be laid off soon, start networking and looking for another position.

Travel
- Visit places that feature reddish earth, rocks and mountains.
- If your family emigrated at some point from your ancestral home, visit it. Connect with relatives there if possible.
- Travel to places of archeological significance.
- Go to see your grandparents or childhood hometown.
- Visit places of great agricultural abundance.
- Go anyplace that makes you feel grounded and secure.

Colors
Red is the color of the first chakra. This can be any shade of red, from deepest crimson to a gentle pink. Wear or bring into your home a shade of red that especially appeals to you. A scarf or vase of flowers is an easy way to incorporate color into your life. Extra points for red

shoes! Bringing shades of red into the family room is also especially beneficial.

Scents

Surround yourself with pleasing, earthy smells, such as cedar, clove or patchouli. Essential oils are a wonderful way to bring these aromas into your life. (Use them in the air, rather than on your skin, unless you know what you're doing—see Appendix 4 for more on how to use essential oils.) You could also just bring some cedar fronds into your home or simmer some cloves in a pan on the stove to fill your home with an earthy, spicy aroma. The scents of rich, loamy earth and baking bread are also very supportive to the first chakra.

Affirmations

(See Appendix 5 for tips on how to work with affirmations.)
Repeat affirmations such as:
- I am safe.
- I have a right to be here.
- I have a right to be me, just as I am.
- I am able to create a safe and nurturing home.
- Life is good.
- I can effortlessly ground to the earth and draw stability, comfort and energetic nourishment from it. (See Appendix 1 for more instructions on how to ground.)
- The universe is a good and benevolent place.
- Everything is going to work out just fine.
- I belong.
- I have all that I need and will continue to have all that I need.
- I can easily and joyfully access the abundance and bounty of the universe.
- All is well. I can let down my guard and rest.

- I am able to create a healthy, secure and loving family environment.
- I am healthy and strong. I draw on an inexhaustible source of vitality and wellbeing.
- I have all the energy required to do the things I want and need to do.

A First Chakra Blessing

May you have abundance, health, family joy, and a sense of contentment and ease deep in your bones.

CHAPTER 10

Second Chakra: Getting In The Flow

Nourish The Source Of Joy, Creativity, Emotion, Pleasure And Life Force

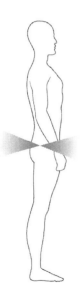

The second chakra, also called the sacral chakra, is located at the lower abdomen/lower back, between the pubic bone and the navel. Like all five middle chakras, it projects out from the body in both front and back.

Its keywords are "life energy" and "creativity." It relates to vitality, sexual/erotic health and fulfillment, emotion, ease with change, creativity, grace, relationships with lovers and mates, fluidity, pleasure and sensation.

Like the first chakra, its functions are very basic and are a necessary foundation for the health and function of the rest of the chakras. Both structure and flow are necessary to any life form, and the second chakra provides flow as the counterpart to the first chakra's structure. Although the emotions governed by the second chakra become more and more highly calibrated as our upper chakras flower, they always remain an important source of information and life force for us. The vitality and creative energy that the second chakra gives us are the basic building blocks for creation, recreation and pro-creation.

Clearing, balancing, and opening the sacral chakra helps us regain our joie de vivre. It gets our life juices and creative juices flowing, and that makes our lives more—well, juicy.

Its color is orange, and its associated element is water.

Second Chakra At A Glance

Common English name	Sacral Chakra
Location	Lower abdomen, lower back
Associations	Sexuality, emotions, eroticism, pleasure, creativity, sensation, flow
Related organs	Reproductive organs, bladder, kidneys, lower back, pelvis
Related sense	Taste
Related color	Orange
Related element	Water
Ideal level of functioning	Sexual/erotic health and fulfillment, passion, ease with change, creativity, grace, fluidity, balanced emotions, joie de vivre

Is Your Second Chakra Healthy?

Someone with a healthy sacral chakra will usually be energetic and eager for whatever is coming next.

You love life! The phrase "joie de vivre" was made for you. You gobble up life and open all your senses to joy.

You are able to be spontaneous and play. Change comes easily to you—you just "go with the flow." Basically, you feel that life goes pretty smoothly for you.

You feel your emotions strongly, but are not overpowered by them. Other people may think of you as warm and emotional, even passionate.

Although you may or may not be beautiful or handsome, there is most likely something attractive about you—a sparkle in your eye, a sense of personal style, a certain something that draws people to you. You may enjoy spas, salons, flattering clothes or other ways of tending your attractiveness.

Your love life will usually be a source of satisfaction and pleasure for you. The solitary life is not for you. You will enjoy your sexuality, without having it rule you.

You'll most likely enjoy luxuries when you can get them—beautiful clothes, sensuous fabrics, smooth-riding cars, massages, a bubble bath, fine art and so on. Food will likely be a source of great pleasure for you and you may especially enjoy sweets and fine wine.

You will enjoy creative expression, and may be either a professional or amateur artist. In any case, you will enjoy the creative efforts of others, and will seek beautiful people, places, objects and experiences. Whether or not you have a lot of money, your home will likely be beautifully decorated and feature sumptuous colors and fabrics, fresh flowers, and, of course, art.

You will be at ease with your senses and sexuality, and your sexual organs, bladder, prostate, womb, kidneys, and lower back will most likely be healthy.

Is Your Second Chakra Out Of Balance?

If your second chakra is out of balance, you just won't feel much joy. Life may seem flat and colorless, all work and no play, like all the juice has been squeezed out of it.

If your second chakra is underactive or blocked, you might be emotionally cold. If it's overactive or open too wide, you might feel that you're at the mercy of your emotions, always being tossed on a turbulent sea of feelings and desires.

If your second chakra is underactive, you might have a low libido and difficulty experiencing pleasure of all kinds. You might fill your days and evenings with work and avoid vacations; spend a lot of time spacing out in front of the TV or video games; deny yourself small pleasures; and live austerely. You may hold back from invitations to do things you'd really like to do. You might have great difficulty with transitions, even staying in situations that aren't good for you just because you fear or dislike change so much.

If it's overactive, you might be overly focused on sexual and physical sensation. This could express itself as over-eating, over-drinking, over-shopping, addiction to pornography or difficulty controlling your sexual impulses. You might be addicted to change, frequently moving, switching jobs or falling in love with someone new.

In either case, whether your second chakra is overactive or underactive, you may have had a history of problems in your love life. You may feel creatively blocked or believe that you're not creative. You may feel clumsy and tell people, "I'm such a klutz." You may feel unattractive and hide your face behind a curtain of hair or envelop your body in bulky fabrics, or on the other hand, you may have a propensity for tastelessly revealing clothes.

You may feel, as a life pattern or just temporarily, that your life isn't going smoothly and that you're constantly running into rough patches, dead ends and problems.

In childhood, you may have been shamed for your body, your sexuality or bladder and bowel control. You may have been sexually molested or abused. In adulthood, this can create an ongoing background feeling of shame.

With regard to your physical body, you may have problems with your lower back, sexual organs, uterus, prostate, kidneys or bladder.

Work With Your Second Chakra If...

In summary, it would benefit you to clear, balance and support growth in your second chakra if more than two or three of these statements apply to you:

- You've been working too hard, either temporarily or as a lifestyle.
- Life feels like a grind.
- You've lost your ability to feel joy, to play, to be creative.
- You feel numb, or your mate complains that you never express your feelings.
- You say things like "It was sinfully delicious."
- You have a hard time with change.
- Things seem difficult and you'd like more of a sense of flow in your life.
- You're unhappy with your erotic life.
- You have a hard time sticking with anything for very long and are always changing to something else.
- You have a sense that you're _too_ focused on sexuality or physical pleasure.
- You deny yourself small pleasures.
- Your home is lacking in decorations, homey touches and creature comforts.
- You'd like more creativity in your life.
- You think of yourself as clumsy.
- You don't like your body.
- You're an artist or dream of being one.
- You want more beauty in your life.

- You have an underlying sense of guilt or shame about your body, your sexuality or your life.
- You don't feel attractive.
- You rarely take time to cultivate your attractiveness.
- You struggle with low-level depression.
- You'd like to develop more physical, social or emotional grace.
- You often feel guilty.
- Your emotions feel overwhelming.
- As a child, you were sexually molested or you grew up in a highly sexually repressive family.
- Your sense of taste is "off."
- Your culture is highly puritanical or sexually repressive.
- You have health issues involving your sexual organs, bladder or kidneys.
- You frequently get bladder or kidney infections.
- You are having difficulty with fertility.
- You often suffer low back pain.

How to Clear, Balance And Nurture Your Second Chakra

Here are some practical, enjoyable, down-to-earth things you can do to support second chakra health and radiance. Of course, you don't have to do them all! Remember, intention is the key thing.

Activities

- Practice calendar therapy. Free up your schedule to make more time for spontaneity and then do fun things on the spur of the moment.
- Flirt (safely and responsibly, of course).
- Dance. Don't be afraid to be sensual with it.
- Swim, especially in the moonlight, if you can manage it.
- Practice small changes. Take a new route home from work. Try a new recipe. Wear a different color or style. Part your hair on the opposite side.
- Make something. Anything will do.
- Do anything that makes you feel graceful.

Physical Body

- Find the bumps that are your anklebones, placing your thumb on one and your fingers on the other. Move them straight back, toward your heel, into the fleshy spot just in front of the Achilles' tendon. Hold these acupressure points for one minute. Hold the acupressure point two finger-widths below your navel for one minute.
- Pamper yourself. Take a nap, have a luxurious bath, get a massage or get your hair or nails done.

- Take extra time to dress in flattering clothes. Adorn yourself in a new way.
- If you haven't been to the doctor in a long time for a women's or men's health exam (in other words, a reproductive organ wellness checkup), make an appointment now.
- Stretch and do other flexibility-building exercises.
- Make love.
- Figure out what your most attractive physical feature is and show it off.

Home

- Surround yourself with beauty—art, flowers, music, color—whatever gives you the elevated feeling that beauty confers. Allow yourself a moment to savor your objects of beauty every time you see or hear them.
- Add something comfortable or luxurious to your home. It can be as big as a new sofa or as small as a fancy bar of soap.
- Play romantic music.
- Enjoy flowers, especially roses, irises and other beautiful-smelling blooms. You can bring a bouquet in or just enjoy them in the garden.
- Get luxurious new sheets for your bed. Make it a cozy, sumptuous nest.
- Add flowing fabrics, soft lighting, plush fabrics and pillows, and lovely scents.
- Turn off the electric lights and light some candles.

Family, Friends and Community

- Set aside some time for romance with your mate or lover.
- If you're not in a relationship and would like to be, take some concrete steps to meet a potential new romantic partner.

- Not feeling romantic? Go out to dinner with (or cook dinner for) a friend who really enjoys food and see if you can match their enjoyment bite for bite.
- Declare a family play-day. Do whatever suits your collective fancy. Fun sensory activities such as making mud pies, blowing bubbles, playing in the sand or picking berries are especially good.
- Change something (with mutual agreement, of course) in routines you've established with family or friends.
- If you're in a committed relationship, introduce something new to your love life.
- Do something with your most fun, spontaneous friend.

Food

Drink plenty of water. Experiment with tasty new beverages. Eat orange fruits and vegetables and produce with a high water content. Enjoy sweets mindfully and in moderation. Make eating a sensual experience and savor every bite of your food.

Work and Career

- Bring some color and beauty into your workplace. A new water feature, such as a small fountain, would be excellent. At the very least, rearrange things at your work station to improve aesthetics and work flow.
- Have you been resisting transitions at work? See if you can adapt a little.
- Brainstorm things, small or large, that can you do to make your job more enjoyable. Pick several and do them.
- See what kind of change you can introduce into your work life. Consider applying for a new job.
- Take a day and go with the flow. Whatever happens, just roll with it.

- If there are processes that don't work smoothly, see what you can do to improve their flow.
- Figure out ways to introduce more fun, creativity and play into your workday.
- Notice where your passions lie—the parts of your work that really get you fired up—and explore ways to expand those areas.

Travel
- Spend time in moonlight and near open water. (Open water in moonlight is doubly good.)
- Visit places that feature orange earth, rocks, or vegetation.
- Lush tropical places are also excellent supports for the second chakra.
- Travel to countries known for their sense of romance.
- Visit cultures known for their devotion to good food.
- What's the most fun place you can think of? Go there!

Colors
Orange is the color of the second chakra. Bring the color orange (whatever shade feels pleasing to you, from brightest tangerine to softest apricot or salmon) into your life, either wearing it or decorating your home or workplace with it. Wearing an orange skirt, pants or low-slung belt or hip-scarf or adding soft orange or coral accents in the bedroom are especially good.

Scents
Use essential oils or perfumes with especially sensual scents, such as musk, ylang ylang, gardenia or sandalwood. Rose, iris, and jasmine are also good. (Use the essential oils environmentally, rather than applying to your skin, unless you are experienced with aromatherapy. See Appendix 4 for more details about using essential oils.)

Affirmations

(See Appendix 5 for tips on how to work with affirmations.)
Repeat affirmations such as:
- Pleasure is an important and necessary part of my life.
- I give myself permission to fully enjoy my sexuality.
- I embrace my unique beauty (or handsomeness or attractiveness).
- The universe is full of sweetness and beauty.
- I am passionate, sparkling, creative and full of zest for life.
- I am able to change with ease and grace.
- I welcome romance, love and good sex.
- I feel a sense of deep wellbeing and comfort with myself.
- I am in touch with my body. I love it and treat it well.
- My life is graceful and pleasurable.
- I allow my emotions to flow through me in a healthy and balanced way.
- Rest, spontaneity and play are a regular part of my healthy life.
- Creating (fill in the blank) nourishes my spirit and brings me joy.
- My desires and appetites are balanced and harmonious.
- I am joyful. I am spontaneous. I am creative.

A Second Chakra Blessing

May you have joy, grace, creativity, pleasure, emotional healing—and fun!

CHAPTER 11

Third Chakra:
Coming From Your Place Of Power

Develop Personal Power And Vitality So You Can Build The Life You Want

The third chakra, also called the solar plexus or navel chakra, is located in the upper abdomen between the navel and the bottom of the sternum (breastbone).

Its keywords are "personal power" and "self-esteem." It relates to ego, will, power, effectiveness, persistence, logic, self-regard and metabolism.

Clearing, balancing and opening the third chakra helps us cultivate vitality, develop a healthy sense of self-worth, stand up for ourselves better, set boundaries, grow as leaders, become more effective, think logically, successfully set and reach goals, and create the lives we want.

Whereas the first chakra is about relating to family and the second chakra is about relating to lovers and mates, the third chakra is about relating to community and work. The third chakra helps to make sure that the needs of the first two chakras are met, while providing a necessary developmental step toward the higher chakras. It provides the spark, the fire, and the vitality for progress. Even when the higher chakras are very developed, the third chakra helps to ground them and keep them from being too ethereal.

The associated color of the solar plexus chakra is yellow and its element is fire.

Third Chakra At A Glance

Common English name	Solar Plexus Chakra
Location	Solar plexus (upper abdomen between navel and sternum)
Associations	Ego, will, metabolism, personal power, personal boundaries, personal identity, logical thought
Related organs	Digestive organs and system, immune system, adrenal glands, muscles
Related sense	Sight
Related color	Yellow
Related element	Fire
Ideal level of functioning	Healthy use of personal power; strong will and perseverance, effectiveness in accomplishing personal goals, healthy boundaries, ample personal energy, strong confidence and self-esteem, ability to think logically

Is Your Third Chakra Healthy?

People with healthy solar plexus chakras will usually have a clear sense of who they are and where they're going. (This will deepen and become more elevated and less ego-based as the fifth chakra evolves.) You have a strong sense of self-worth and self-trust. Because of this, you are decisive and effective at reaching goals and getting what you want.

You have a healthy relationship to power—neither dominating others nor letting yourself be dominated. Other people probably think of you as assertive. You use power well, often rising to leadership positions.

You are able to take reasonable risks, when there is a reason to do so, and are confident in your ability to handle problems as they arise. You are able to think clearly and logically.

You accept that some stress is an inevitable part of life, but you manage it well. You take care of yourself and get enough rest and down time. You know that you are more effective if your life is balanced. You usually have a steady, sustainable supply of physical vitality.

You respect yourself and it shows in your posture, clothing and manner of speaking. You know what you want, and within reason, expect to get it.

You maintain personal boundaries well. People know where they stand with you, and you likely have a reputation for being firm and direct. In a group, you make sure your voice is heard and your needs are met. When you get angry, you express and channel it in constructive ways. You are willing to fight for things you value, but only when it is necessary. You maintain your power in a quiet but firm way.

You have a knack for making things happen. You can take an idea and make it into a reality, whether that's a meal, a doghouse, a vacation, or something grander such as a business, organization or solution to a world problem.

You usually have sound digestive, immune and muscular systems. You tend to be free of major allergies, hypertension, diabetes and adrenal gland disorders. Your weight and height will usually be in healthy proportion.

Is Your Third Chakra Out Of Balance?

If your third chakra is out of balance, you will often feel a sense of powerlessness. You may feel that you just can't get traction on some of the important things in your life. It may be difficult for you to get what you want or to make things happen.

If your third chakra is underactive or blocked, you may feel overlooked and unnoticed—that "What am I, a potted plant?" feeling. In a group, it may be very hard for you to speak up. If you do speak, you may find that no one hears you or that they talk right over you.

You will probably lack confidence and self-esteem. You may have a "victim mentality," feeling that others tend to mistreat you. You may be submissive. You may not have a clear or strong personality. You may not have a sense of where you're going in life and what you want to accomplish. If people ask you what you want, you may have a hard time responding. You may shun leadership, responsibility and decision-making.

Clear, logical thinking may be difficult for you and you may be easily manipulated by others.

If your third chakra is overactive or open too wide, you may be bossy or domineering. In a group, you may talk too much, imposing your will on others. You may misuse power, taking pleasure in showing others that you have power over them. You may even be a bully.

In either case, whether your third chakra is overactive or underactive, in order to get things done you may rely on your personal will to an excessive degree, pulling energy primarily out of your own energy system rather than relying on the natural rhythms of your body and receiving energy from the earth and the cosmos. You work too hard and end up exhausted. You may have immune system problems, get sick frequently or be plagued with a chronic sense of fatigue. Stress may cause you emotional and physical misery.

Often this excessive work comes from a basic sense of unworthiness. You may feel that you have to work extremely hard or achieve amazing things in order to be worthy of love and respect. You may be very hard on yourself, expecting perfection.

As a child, may have been required to be strictly obedient, repress anger and submit to power.

Your posture may be slumped and submissive, head and eyes down. Conversely, if your third chakra is overactive, you may have a chest-out, chin-jutting, domineering posture.

With regard to your physical body, you may have problems with digestion, such as irritable bowel syndrome, Crohn's disease, etc. Your immune system may be overactive, resulting in allergies and immune system disorders, or underactive, resulting in frequent illnesses. You may have diabetes, hypertension, ulcers or adrenal gland issues.

Work With Your Third Chakra If...

In summary, it would benefit you to clear, balance and support growth in your third chakra if several of these statements apply to you:

- You lack confidence in yourself.
- You experience problems with digestion.
- You have significant allergies.
- You have a chronic sense of unworthiness.
- Making decisions is hard for you.
- You have trouble speaking up in a group, or when you do speak up no one takes notice.
- You either refuse to take part in conflict or you are too willing to get into a fight.
- You feel like you rarely get what you want.
- You have issues with anger–either repressing it or expressing it too violently.
- It is difficult for you to "get things off the drawing board" and make things happen.
- You tend to blindly follow authority.
- You don't really know what you want out of life.
- You are a member of a group or class that your culture disempowers and represses.
- Taking risks scares you so much you avoid it at all costs; or conversely, you often take unnecessary risks.
- You're very hard on yourself, holding yourself to extremely strict standards.
- You work so hard to reach goals that you disregard your own health.
- You feel like others push you around.

- As a child your boundaries were routinely violated or your parents were excessively strict and repressive.
- Others tell you that you're too domineering or bossy.
- You often feel stressed.
- You are often ill.
- You habitually breathe into your chest (top of your lungs), rather than your belly (filling your lungs fully).
- You wish you could step up to a leadership role.
- You feel like a victim.
- Taking power seems scary or bad.
- You're exhausted from always trying too hard.
- You overeat or over-drink to relieve stress.
- You've recently received a major blow to your self-esteem.
- You'd like to be more assertive, in a constructive way.
- You'd like to think more clearly and logically.

How to Clear, Balance And Nurture Your Third Chakra

Here are some practical, "hands-on" things you can do to support third chakra health and radiance. Of course, you don't have to do them all—just choose the ones that resonate with you. And remember, intention is the key to making them really work.

Activities
- Roar like a lion.
- Set a feasible goal. Break it down into distinct, doable steps. Make a timeline for finishing each step. Take a first step to set the process in motion. Follow through with your timeline so that you reach your goal on time. Then celebrate how powerful and effective you are!
- Assert yourself. Make sure your voice is heard and your needs are taken into account. If this is hard for you, start small. For example, YOU decide what restaurant you'll go to or what movie you'll see. This may feel uncomfortable to you, but with practice it'll get easier.
- Spend time in the sunlight. (Protect yourself from sunburn, of course.)
- Participate in a vigorous sport or activity. Trust yourself and play to win.
- Clean out a messy closet or do another task that you've been putting off. Make sure to choose something that you can finish.
- Make a special effort to dress and groom yourself well. Get a great haircut and wear clothes that proclaim your self-respect.
- Remember to hold your head high.

Physical Body

- Belly breathe. This balances the third chakra with each breath. At the same time, belly breathing supports the nervous system, the adrenal glands and the immune system. (See Appendix 3 for instructions.)
- Hold the acupressure point "Three Mile Point" on the outside of your upper calves, about four finger-widths below the kneecap, in the depression between the shinbone and the muscle.
- Pay attention to your body and emotions. Rest when you need to.
- Laugh. Sing. Both of these are great stress relievers.
- Take a stress management class.
- Assume a confident, powerful posture and maintain it for at least 90 seconds.
- Do strength-building exercises.

Home

- Spruce up your home office or gym. If you don't have rooms dedicated to work and exercise, at least create comfortable, efficient spaces for these functions.
- Clean your bathroom and put out new towels.
- If you have a fence around your property, repair any gaps.
- Display objects or pictures that speak to you of personal power used for good purposes.
- Make a maintenance plan for your house.
- Upgrade the electrical systems.
- Make improvements to the front of your home. Add touches that give your home a "house-proud" look.

Family, Friends and Community

- Take on a project or problem in your neighborhood or community. Assume leadership and make your goal happen.

- Join the board of a community organization. Support justice in your community.
- Within your family, be a good role model for work-life balance and stress management.
- Be direct in your dealings with family and friends.
- Learn to deal with anger in healthy ways.
- Watch funny movies with family and friends.
- Spend time with friends who make you feel good about yourself.

Food

Enjoy healthy complex carbohydrates, such as whole grains, legumes and potatoes. Cut back on sugar. Use alcohol and stimulants moderately or not at all. Make sure you take time for each meal, sit down to eat and chew your food well. Don't allow your mealtimes to be interrupted.

Work and Career

- Let other people know immediately when they've stepped on your toes.
- Make a 5-year career growth plan for yourself, with concrete steps for reaching those goals.
- Take a public speaking class. Give a presentation.
- Take assertiveness training.
- Learn to prioritize tasks. Focus on getting the top priorities done, then quit at quitting time.
- Ask for a raise, giving concrete examples of why you deserve it.
- If you'd like to feel more challenged, step up and take on a new responsibility. If you have more responsibilities than you can comfortably handle, figure out a way to let some of them go.
- If you're a workaholic, take steps to bring greater balance between work and the rest of your life.

Travel

- Visit dry settings with lots of light and warmth, such as deserts or grasslands.
- Spend time in areas with an overall yellow tone in the earth, rocks or vegetation.
- Visit volcanoes or other sites that emanate a lot of geologic or thermal power.
- Go to locations that are related to your career or hoped-for career.
- Tour centers of world power.
- Travel to places associated with your personal heroes.
- Visit areas associated with cultures past or present that have achieved great worldly accomplishments.

Colors

The color of the third chakra is yellow—from chrome yellow, to soft butter yellow, to the mellow tan of dry grass. Wear or decorate a room in a shade of yellow that is pleasing and energizing to you. Particularly appropriate would be wearing a yellow or tan belt or vest, or bringing yellow or a rich tan into your home office, gym or other personal spaces. Use the color with a sense of purpose and intention, feeling it energizing your third chakra.

Scents

Use strong, assertive scents such as cinnamon, ginger, peppermint or juniper, or crisp scents such as lemon or lemongrass. It's likely that you already have many of these in your kitchen. You can also use essential oils, but use them environmentally, rather than on your skin unless you are familiar with aromatherapy. (See Appendix 4 for more information on using essential oils.)

Affirmations

(See Appendix 5 for tips on how to work with affirmations.)
Repeat affirmations such as:
- I am powerful and capable. I effectively manifest the deep desires of my soul.
- I set and reach my goals.
- I, and only I, am in charge of my life.
- I have abundant energy.
- What I've done is good enough.
- If conflict is necessary, I can take it on. I can resolve differences with assertiveness, fairness and open-mindedness.
- I can solve any problem that comes up.
- I make good decisions and act with confidence, purpose and persistence.
- I am a natural leader.
- I love and respect myself.
- I can do this!
- I am worthy of the best in life.
- I rest when I need to. I keep my work in balance with the rest of my life.
- I stand up for myself and what I believe in.
- My needs are important. I am a strong advocate for myself and my needs.

A Third Chakra Blessing

May you have a clear sense of your infinite worth, the knowledge that the deep desires of your soul matter enormously, and an understanding that you are an immensely powerful being who can manifest those deep, sacred desires.

CHAPTER 12

Fourth Chakra: Heart Wisdom

Open To Healing, Meaningful Relationships, Self-Compassion, And Universal Love

The fourth chakra, also called the heart chakra, is located in the center of the chest at heart level. Its keywords are "unconditional love," "healing," and "connection."

The heart chakra relates to compassion, healing, relationships and love—unconditional love of others, love of self and divine love. The love that characterizes the fourth chakra comes from a deep and sacred source and brings with it a sense of inner peace.

Situated at the middle of the chakra system (with three chakras above and three below), the fourth chakra integrates the upper and lower chakras. It unifies body and spirit.

With the fourth chakra, we start to move beyond the focus on ego and the separate self, toward a focus on relationship and connection. At the heart chakra, the spiritual self begins to truly emerge.

With divine love as its model, on an earthly level the heart chakra supports healthy, unconditionally loving relationships—loving the divine in human form. This includes an emotionally healthy parent's love of her or his children, a deep and true friendship, unselfish love for a mate or romantic partner and any other relationship that goes beyond being purely romantic, sentimental, physical or self-interested. The heart chakra also supports compassion for others near and far.

On a spiritual level, the heart chakra dissolves the feeling of separateness and aloneness in the universe and helps us feel integrated and whole in body, mind, emotions and spirit. It helps us feel connected to whatever we hold sacred and dear. It also helps us to feel deeply linked to and nourished by nature.

Its color is green and its related element is air.

Fourth Chakra At A Glance

Common English name	Heart Chakra
Location	Center of chest at heart level
Associations	Love, integration, self-love, compassion, healing, relationships, connection to nature, connection to universal/divine love
Related organs	Lungs, thymus, heart, respiratory & cardiac systems, arms, hands
Related sense	Touch
Related color	Green
Related element	Air
Ideal level of functioning	Ability to feel compassion, ability to love deeply and unconditionally, healthy self-love, healthy or healing intimate relationships, sense of connection and being loved, inner peace, no barriers to healing, strong relationship with the natural world

Is Your Fourth Chakra Healthy?

Someone with a healthy fourth chakra is usually compassionate and able to love deeply.

In relationships, you are capable of deep intimacy. You are kind, forgiving, trusting, openhearted, nonjudgmental and capable of unconditional love (or as close as most of us can get in this human form). Even if your heart gets broken, you are willing to let it heal and love again.

You probably have a good sense of what others are feeling and have compassion for them. However, you are able to keep a healthy separation in most cases. You will naturally maintain healthy emotional boundaries and lovingly encourage others to do the same. In other words, you won't be a person who "loves too much." You will be able to balance giving and receiving in your relationships and equitably and flexibly share the role of caregiver.

You also have a healthy amount self-love, appreciating your own essential worthiness and strengths while being able to accept and forgive your mistakes and flaws.

You probably have a strong connection to nature and love animals. Many people with healthy fourth chakras (though certainly not all) love the outdoors and have animal companions (pets).

Involvement in the helping or healing professions is common, but whatever your occupation, you act as a healing presence. You're probably generous and may volunteer in the community. You're known as someone who can be counted on when a friend is in need.

You are likely to have a spiritual aspect to your life, and it is richly sustaining to you. You may often radiate peace.

You probably have healthy lungs, heart, respiratory and cardiac systems, thymus gland, arms and hands.

Is Your Fourth Chakra Out Of Balance?

If your fourth chakra is out of balance, you will be out of alignment with your heart.

Someone with a blocked or underactive fourth chakra may feel intense loneliness and lack of emotional fulfillment. You might have difficulty accepting or giving love. You may hold grudges and find it hard to forgive others for human imperfections and errors large and small. You may lack compassion and others might think of you as cold-hearted. Your close relationships may wither on the vine for lack of love. You may be uncomfortable with intimacy and touch.

On the other hand, if your fourth chakra is overactive or overly open, you may have a pattern of unhealthy relationships in which you "love too much" and give too much of yourself, or in which you are clingy and highly possessive. Your sense of personal boundaries may be distorted and you may both intrude on others and allow others to intrude on you. (This could also indicate an imbalanced third chakra. Chakra issues are often inter-related.) If you are an empath (meaning that you feel the feelings of other people), you may be overwhelmed by the painful emotions of others.

In either case, whether your heart chakra is over- or underactive, your relationships are likely to be characterized by love that is not of the highest form.

You will likely have difficulty with self-love and self-compassion. You may show kindness and forgiveness to others but not to yourself.

Heartbreak and grief may be difficult for you to recover from. Your life may be tinged with sorrow and emotional pain.

You may lack a sustaining connection to a higher power. You may feel unmoved by the beauty of nature and have little desire to be out in it. You may be out of touch with or unkind to your body.

As a child, you may have had your emotional boundaries routinely violated. You may have been emotionally neglected, or have felt unloved. A parent may have died or abandoned you. Your parents may have been very emotionally needy or have had issues with alcohol or other addictive substances. They may have separated in an unhealthy way (for them or for you). You may have lived in a household that was emotionally shallow.

You may have problems with your heart, lungs, circulatory system, arms or hands. Your shoulders may be rounded and your chest may appear sunken or collapsed. Your upper back may frequently cause you pain. Asthma, pneumonia or other respiratory issues may be problems for you. You may suffer from depression.

Work With Your Fourth Chakra If...

In summary, it would benefit you to clear, balance and support growth in your fourth chakra if more than two or three of the following statements apply to you:

- There's an important relationship in your life that you're having trouble with.
- You're lonely or have a hard time connecting to others in a meaningful way.
- You have an emotional wound that won't heal.
- There's someone (including yourself) you'd like to forgive.
- You're tired of shallow relationships and would like to form a deep and meaningful bond with someone.
- You would describe yourself as feeling alienated or isolated.
- You are in a healing or therapeutic profession (or would like to be).
- You are out of touch with or unkind to your body.
- You're on a path of spiritual growth.
- You'd like to rise to a higher level of compassion and non-judgment for others or for yourself.
- You are grieving.
- Others have told you that you have problems with commitment.
- You want to feel more connected to nature.
- You want to feel more connected to a sense of sacredness or to your spiritual source/higher power.
- You've recently experienced heartbreak.
- One or both parents were alcoholic or had other addiction problems.

- Life generally seems sad and painful.
- You sense that you need healing on a deep level.
- You'd like to rise above anger, hatred and jealousy.
- Someone has hurt you deeply, or vice versa.
- You have asthma or other breathing difficulties.
- You have difficulty with intimacy and touch.
- You are part of a culture that strongly values individualism.
- You were abandoned or emotionally neglected as a child or had a parent who died while you were still dependent on them.
- Your upper back often hurts.
- You've had pneumonia more than once.
- You've never experienced unconditional love (or anything close to it).
- You have respiratory, circulatory or heart problems.
- You are an intuitive empath (i.e. you feel the feelings of others).
- You give your heart away too easily and "love too much," or you drive people away because you are clingy and possessive. (Also work with your third chakra if this is true for you.)

How to Clear, Balance And Nurture Your Fourth Chakra

Here are some practical, enjoyable, commonsense things you can do to support fourth chakra health and radiance. Of course, you don't have to do them all! Once you see the pattern, I'm sure you'll be able to think of more. Remember, intention is the "secret ingredient."

Activities

- Do your best to forgive someone. Whatever it is or was that they did, just let it go.
- Perform a "random act of kindness" every day for a week. Notice how it makes you feel. (However, if your fourth chakra is overactive and you routinely give too much, aim that act of kindness at yourself.)
- Make a list of everyone you can think of, living or dead, who loves you or has loved you. Love is always current, always present, even when a relationship has "ended" or a person has died. Open your heart and let the love sink in. Try to keep the awareness of being loved in the forefront of your heart all day, like a warm glow.
- Declare a "gratitude day." Spend the whole day noticing everything that you have to be grateful for. If you find yourself slipping into any attitude or frame of mind that isn't gratitude, gently guide yourself back. In your journal, write down your "gratitudes." Express thanks and appreciation to as many people as you can. Go to sleep grateful.
- Find a place that feels sacred to you and visit it often.
- If your parents had substance abuse issues, seek help and support.
- If you are grieving, seek support.

Physical Body

- Place your hands over your heart and hold them there for five minutes or so.
- Gently thump your mid-chest, over your thymus gland, for a minute or so.
- Hold the acupressure point The Sea of Tranquility, in the center of your chest about three and a half finger-widths above the base of your sternum (breast-bone).
- Laugh.
- If your health permits, do some aerobic exercise.
- Pull your shoulders back.
- Do the yoga pose "the cobra."
- Get your heart, lungs and blood pressure checked.
- If you are depressed, seek professional help.

Home

- Bring greenery or plants into your home or paint a wall a soothing shade of green or pink.
- Clean and de-clutter your kitchen.
- Think of one thing you can do to make your home a more loving place. Do that. Repeat.
- Put up pictures of loved ones or heart-centered spiritual teachers.
- Bake bread. Cook nourishing food.
- Share a meal with loved ones.
- If you have a fireplace, build a fire and sit in front of it.

Family, Friends and Community

- Spend time with small children and animal companions. Get down on their level. Follow their lead. (Most dogs have a lot to teach us about unconditional love and can be great models for opening our heart chakras.)

- Reconnect with an old, dear friend or two. Let them know what they've meant to you.
- If you have children, hug them and tell them you love them at least several times a day. (Perhaps less for teenagers, but find a way to convey your love every day!)
- If you are part of a spiritual community that is enriching to you, participate in it.
- If your heart chakra is underactive, volunteer at a food bank, pet shelter or homeless shelter. Withhold judgment and try to learn something from and see the divine spark within everyone you seek to help. Smile at people on the street. Express appreciation freely. Do something genuinely nice for your spouse or significant other without expecting payback.
- If your fourth chakra is overactive, take time for yourself. Practice setting limits. Say no to an overly needy friend. Ask for help. Accept all compliments and offers of help. Think of ways to be more loving and kind to yourself.

Food

Enjoy vegetables and comforting, soothing dishes that are not overly rich. Avoid heavy fats and foods that are bad for your heart and circulatory system. Avoid alcohol and addictive substances, even sugar. Prepare food with loving thoughts and try to consume only those foods that were made lovingly.

Work and Career

- If there is strife or a rift in your work community, consider what you can do to heal it. Be a uniter.
- Let go of a grudge.
- If someone is being picked on or gossiped about, refuse to take part in it.

- Recommit to being part of a team.
- Bring a live green plant into your workspace.
- Put up photos of family, friends or animal companions.
- Get out and take a walk during lunch to support the health of your physical heart.
- If you're the "office mother" try stepping out of that role. If you're the office grump, make an effort to be friendlier.

Travel
- Spend time in any natural setting. Forests and other places with lots of greenery are especially good.
- Visit loving family and friends.
- Take a service vacation (unless you are an "over-giver.")
- Visit places associated with healing.
- Visit cultures known for open-heartedness and non-materialism.
- Go anywhere that gives you a deep feeling of connectedness and belonging.

Colors
The color of the heart chakra is green, from deep emerald to a light, airy spring green. Pink is also associated with the heart chakra. Wear or decorate a room in a shade of green or pink that feels pleasing and healing to you. Bringing green or pink into the kitchen, either through paint, decorations or plants, or wearing a pink or green shirt or pendant is especially helpful.

Scents
Use the heart chakra scents of rose, geranium, neroli, melissa, sandalwood, chamomile or jasmine. These can be from the garden or in the form of essential oils. (Don't use essential oils directly on the skin un-

less you are experienced with aromatherapy. See Appendix 4 for more information.)

Affirmations

(See Appendix 5 for tips on how to work with affirmations.)
Repeat affirmations such as:
- I forgive naturally and easily.
- It is my nature to love and be loved.
- I welcome the differences of others. I accept others as they are.
- I give and receive freely and in balance.
- I maintain healthy emotional boundaries.
- I have a genius for healthy, deep, meaningful relationships.
- Love is everywhere. I see and feel love all around me. My heart is full.
- I am fully open to receiving love.
- My body, mind and heart have a genius for healing. It is my nature to heal.
- I love and forgive myself.
- Nature is a source of infinite renewal and healing for me.
- I am at peace.
- I have so much to be grateful for.
- The love that I give comes back to me many times over.
- I am connected to everything in the universe. I am never alone.

A Fourth Chakra Blessing

May you have abundant love and compassion, flowing both in to and out from you, in a never-ending, radiant stream. May you experience the sea of love in which your being floats. May you feel your essential connection to all things.

CHAPTER 13

Fifth Chakra: Who Are You, Really?

Speak Your Truth, Walk Your Path, Create From Your Essence

The fifth chakra, also called the throat chakra, is located (not surprisingly) in the throat. Its keywords are "self-expression," "creativity," "communication" and "truth."

The fifth chakra governs our ability to express ourselves, speak the truth and create.

Each of us has a life path, something that we are called to do. The throat chakra helps us get on that path and stay on it. It supports us in maintaining personal integrity and expressing the fullness of who we are—our most whole, most sacred selves. It helps us bring our personal essence into the physical world, expressing our unique perspective on life. It allows us to create, and in doing so, to activate and express our unique natures.

The fifth chakra is a critical element in spiritual development. Living with integrity about who we really are helps prepare us for greater wisdom and personal growth. In this way, the fifth chakra is important for developing the sixth and seventh chakras.

Speaking our truth and revealing our essence, rather than hiding behind a protective mask, also encourages others to evolve. Truth is an evolutionary force!

The fifth chakra's associated color is sky blue. Its element is sound.

Fifth Chakra At A Glance

Common English name	Throat Chakra
Location	Center of throat
Associations	Communication, self-expression, creativity, truth, authenticity
Related organs	Throat and neck, mouth, ears, nose, sinuses, bronchial tubes, thyroid and parathyroid glands, shoulders
Related sense	Hearing
Related color	Light blue
Related element	Sound
Ideal level of functioning	Ability to express one self and manifest personal essence in the world, clear communication, speaking one's truth, honesty and integrity, rich creative life

Is Your Fifth Chakra Healthy?

Someone with a healthy throat chakra will usually be able to create a distinctive and fulfilling life.

You are very in touch with yourself and what is true for you. You will probably have a very good sense of when you are "on track" or "off track" in your life. The life you create for yourself may not look conventional, unless that is what is truly right for you.

You are a good listener and often an effective speaker or writer, too. Because of your knack for clear communication, (especially if your heart chakra is also well developed), your relationships are probably pretty harmonious. However, you may be impatient with shallow conversation and affected or inauthentic people.

People usually know where they stand with you. You know what is true for you and realize that everyone is usually best served by directness. However, with your finely honed communication skills, your expression of your perspective tends to be diplomatic and constructive. You are likely known for this tactful honesty, and for having a knack for getting to the underlying truth of matters.

Your work may involve communication, either written or spoken. You may enjoy teaching and sharing your knowledge and skills. With your strong sense of self and your potent ability to communicate, you may be influential or inspirational to others.

You probably have a rich creative life. You may be a professional or serious amateur visual artist, poet, actor or musician. However, it's important to recognize that creativity takes many forms, not expressing itself only through the arts. Your robust creativity could show up in any form, in any part of your life.

You may have a pleasing voice, and will usually have a healthy neck, shoulders, mouth, ears, nose, sinuses and thyroid gland.

Is Your Fifth Chakra Out Of Balance?

If your fifth chakra is out of balance, you will be out alignment with the essence of who you are and what you are meant to do in this life.

Communication may be a major issue for you. You may talk a lot without saying much of value (overactive or too-open fifth chakra), or talk very little at all (underactive or blocked fifth chakra). In either case, you will have difficulty communicating ideas of substance, value and truth.

You probably find it hard to express yourself. You may be indirect, passive-aggressive, extremely shy or just unwilling to speak and share. You might be burning to say things, but the words just won't come out, or other people may frequently misunderstand what you say. Because communication is such an important aspect of life, you may feel out of harmony with others.

With an extremely blocked throat chakra, you may be deceptive, either to yourself or to others. People may think of you as insincere, inauthentic or even untrustworthy.

You may have little motivation to create anything on your own. Consequently, your life may be dominated by consuming the ideas and products of others and may look extremely conventional. This is never satisfying on a deep level, so you will probably feel an emptiness or deep dissatisfaction with your life.

If you are an artist or artisan, a temporarily blocked throat chakra can express itself as a creative block.

You may easily get off track in your life, having no real internal truth by which to steer your way. You may be easily influenced by others.

You may consistently tell yourself and others negative and limiting stories about yourself, such as "I never have any luck," or "No matter what I do I can't make money," or "I'm just unlucky in love."

As a child, you may have been silenced or the adults in your life may have taken little time to listen to you. You may have felt unheard. Your perceptions or truths may have been unwelcome. There may have been family secrets that were never spoken of, even if they were in plain sight. You may have seen your parents living lives that were extremely at odds with the values they professed to hold.

The muscles in your shoulders, neck and throat may be tight, knotted and painful. You may hold your neck in an extremely forward, rather than upright position. You may get frequent sore throats. Your voice may be too soft, overly loud, choked or pinched. You may have problems with your thyroid gland, mouth, ears, nose, sinuses or teeth.

Work With Your Fifth Chakra If...

In summary, it would benefit you to clear, balance and support growth in your fifth chakra if several or more of these statements apply to you:

- You feel that your life doesn't reflect who you really are.
- You'd like to feel more creative.
- You are having trouble speaking your truth and saying the things that need to be said.
- You have recently been silenced about something that matters to you (or were silenced about something major at any time in your life).
- Your life feels too bland.
- You talk too much.
- You'd like to express yourself more clearly and eloquently.
- You feel like no one understands you.
- As a child, you were frequently hushed or told to "shut up!"
- You're an artist or would like to be.
- You're having issues with hearing others' truths or with others hearing your truths.
- You have the nagging sense that you're "off-path" in your life.
- You are indirect, manipulative or passive-aggressive in your communication patterns.
- You'd like to be better at making public speeches or presentations.
- You are a singer or other vocal performer.
- You often second-guess and doubt yourself.
- You live in a repressive culture or are part of a group or class of people that is silenced or not heard.

- You grew up in a household with unspoken secrets.
- You are experiencing a creative block.
- You are uncomfortably shy.
- Conversations with others are feeling dull and lifeless.
- You have recently told or been told a major lie.
- You feel as if you live your life behind a mask and would like to have more of your true self shine through.
- You tell negative or limiting stories about yourself.
- You'd like to prepare yourself for further personal growth and deeper levels of insight.
- Your voice is too soft, too loud, shaky or pinched.
- You have hearing problems.
- You have frequent sore throats or sinus problems.
- You have thyroid problems.
- Your shoulders or neck are frequently tense or painful, or you would say that you "hold your stress" in your neck or shoulders.

How to Clear, Balance And Nurture Your Fifth Chakra

Here are some practical, "real-world" things you can do to support fifth chakra health and radiance. Of course, just choose the ones that resonate with you. Once you see the pattern, I'm sure you'll be able to think of more. Remember that intention is the critical ingredient.

Activities

- Write in your journal. After you've written about something, silently or out loud say "And the truth is..." and then write about the same thing at a deeper level of truth. Continue this process as long as it feels fruitful.
- Sing, hum, or chant. Find a place where you won't be disturbed (preferably one with great resonance), and do it with as much authenticity as you can—with your true voice, not your voice as you think it should sound.
- Listen to someone with you whole self for five minutes; then switch and have him or her listen to you. Both of you should aim for complete presence and should not comment on what the other is saying.
- Speak up about something that you've been silent about. Speak your truth! (For example: write that letter to the editor; ask the question instead of just wondering; speak out about what you normally only mutter under your breath.)
- If you generally dominate conversations, for a whole day try to speak as little as possible and listen as much as you can.
- Create something. Display it or perform it: make sure that others see or hear your creation.

- Read the book *The Artist's Way* and do the exercises in it..
- Do you recognize your inner voice when it speaks? Make a practice of listening for it.

Physical Body

- Hold the acupressure points called Gall Bladder 20 for at least a minute. You'll find them at back of your neck on either side of the spine, just below where your neck meets your skull, in the depressions between the two vertical neck muscles. Tilt your head back and press firmly into these indentations with your thumbs. Your thumbs will be two to three inches apart depending on your size.
- Get a massage focused on your neck, upper back and shoulders.
- If it's been a while since you've had a dental or hearing checkup, make an appointment.
- Do shoulder and neck rolls and the yoga facial exercise known as "the lion."
- Exercise your voice. Take it through its whole range.
- If you have any concerns about your thyroid gland, see a naturopath to have it checked.
- Guard your hearing from ear-damaging, too-loud noises.

Home

- Put in a skylight or enlarge a window so that you can see the sky easily.
- If your home feels a little bland, spice it up with decorations or other elements that are uniquely you. Let your home express your essence.
- Spend time listening closely to all the sounds in your environment.
- Improve your sound system. If external sounds intrude on your home, see what you can do to improve the situation, such as in-

stalling double-paned windows or planting a high hedge to buffer outside noise.
- Make your home a celebration of creativity. Dedicate a room or an area for playing with art supplies or other creative hobbies.
- Display things that you've made.
- Play or make music.

Family, Friends and Community
- If your fifth chakra is overactive, support others in speaking their truth and expressing themselves.
- If your fifth chakra is underactive, make an effort to speak up more. Share your opinion, a truth, how it is for you, or just talk about anything at all!
- Support the arts in your community.
- Make a commitment to telling the truth, kindly and tactfully. Be your authentic self and protect your integrity.
- Honor the creative expressions of your loved ones. Go to their performances, look at their pictures, let them know that you value their unique perspectives and expressions.
- Seek friends who communicate with clarity, truth and integrity.
- Take an art, writing or singing class and let yourself play. Hang out with other creative people.
- If your family's going every which-way, set up a communication/scheduling center and plan regular family dinners at which everyone will be present.

Food
Fruit is the food associated with the fifth chakra. Eat plenty of it. You may also want to eat honey, sea vegetables, and soup. Get creative in the kitchen. Abstain from harmful foods and substances. If you've been thinking of quitting smoking, now is the time.

Work and Career

- Try to incorporate more creative tasks into your workday.
- Take a workshop or read a book on improving workplace communication. Expand your vocabulary.
- In meetings, make sure your voice is heard. Also, be an advocate for others who find it hard to speak up.
- Take on a role that requires public presentations.
- Always be your most honest and above-board self. Value your integrity above all else.
- Take a test that evaluates your core strengths or personality. Do you agree?
- Reconnect with your core values and evaluate whether your job or career furthers those values. If it does, recommit to being part of a team working in service to those values. If it doesn't, consider looking for another job.

Travel

- Visit a place known for its big, blue sky. Bask in it. Breathe the color in, feeling your throat chakra being bathed and nourished.
- Visit an area known for the light blue color of its lakes or ocean.
- Go to places that offer beautiful sounds, either natural or human-made.
- Go to areas celebrated for music.
- Visit centers of creative activity or achievement.
- Go to places known for the distinctiveness of their cultures.

Colors

Light blue is the color of the fifth chakra. Wear or decorate your home with a shade of light blue that feels pleasing and healing to you. A blue scarf or necklace is perfect for this, or bring light blue into your living room, computer room, music room or any area of your house where you build, create or express things.

Scents

Use the scents of lavender, frankincense, sage, clary sage, eucalyptus, or the combinations orange-ylang ylang or cinnamon-vanilla. (If you are using essential oils, use them environmentally rather than applying them directly to your skin unless you are familiar with aromatherapy. See Appendix 4 for more information.) Smelling horseradish is also good for clearing the nose and sinuses. Be careful: it's very strong!

Affirmations

(See Appendix 5 for tips on how to work with affirmations.)
Repeat affirmations such as:
- I allow the truth to speak through me.
- I am heard.
- I have a powerful voice.
- I have the courage to create and live a life that is unique.
- Creativity flows powerfully through me.
- It is my essence to create.
- When I listen I hear the truth of what people are saying.
- I am able to speak to others clearly and eloquently.
- I embrace and celebrate my creativity.
- I live with integrity and lead an authentic life.
- My creativity is welcomed and appreciated.
- I have the courage to tell the truth.
- It is good, right and safe for me to express my true self.
- My truth is necessary.
- I allow my true self, my essence, to be expressed in my life.

A Fifth Chakra Blessing

May you hear and speak truth. May your life and your creations express the fullness of who you are. May you know ever-deeper levels of truth.

CHAPTER 14

Sixth Chakra: The Extraordinary Eye

Expand Clarity, Wisdom And Intuition

The sixth chakra, also called the brow chakra or the third eye, is located in the forehead between and slightly above the eyebrows. Its keywords are "insight," "intellect" and "intuition." The sixth of the seven chakras governs our intellectual and intuitive abilities and our potential for spiritual awareness.

The chakra of mind, it helps us think clearly, but goes beyond this to transcend mere intellect and achieve a deeper level of knowing: wisdom.

It also helps us see clearly, both physically and psychically. It supports imagination, awareness of the subtle/energetic world, intuitive knowing and inner vision. When you see something "with your mind's eye," you are seeing it with the sixth chakra.

The sixth chakra gives us perspective. When it is clear, balanced and highly developed, it makes us like an eagle or hawk, flying high above the surface of the earth. We can see what's happening on the ground, but we're not drawn into it unless we want to be. We're able to stay out of the petty problems and squabbles, trauma and drama, that for many people are the sum and substance of life.

The sixth chakra, when highly developed, leads us out of the darkness. It elevates consciousness and confers deep spiritual insight and awareness. Perception of non-ordinary reality may accompany this. The third eye chakra is crucial to ongoing spiritual development. Thus, keeping it clear and balanced is very important.

Its associated color is indigo and its element is light.

Sixth Chakra At A Glance

Common English Name	Brow Chakra (Third Eye)
Location	Forehead, between and slightly above the eyebrows
Associations	Sight, both physical and intuitive/psychic; intellect; insight; intuition
Related organs	Eyes, brow, brain, pineal gland
Related sense	Sixth sense/intuition
Related color	Indigo
Related element	Light
Ideal level of functioning	Clear, higher-level thought, insight, understanding, perspective, strong intuition, imagination, ability to see clearly both literally and figuratively, wisdom, psychic or subtle-energy awareness

Is Your Sixth Chakra Healthy?

Someone with a healthy brow chakra will have a keen intellect balanced with strong intuitive abilities. This might be summed up as "wisdom." Although you may not express it in conventional forms, you have highly developed ethical and spiritual sensibilities.

A strong sixth chakra often confers the ability to "grasp the big picture," as well as that prized but elusive thing called "vision." As a result, you may be someone who hears and answers the call to greater justice in the world or otherwise seeks to make her or his community, country or world a better place.

You mind works with great clarity. People may think of you as wise and turn to you for insight and advice. You have a high-level perspective that allows you to see patterns and make sense of things that are baffling to others.

You tend to take a long view of things. Having a sense of perspective usually keeps you above the fray: though you are not at all coldhearted, you are able to keep yourself out of most petty conflicts and dramas and avoid getting tangled up in the problems of others. You are likely very fair and able to avoid being judgmental. You're more likely to become amused than irritated or angry. This usually makes for a fairly peaceful, even-keeled life. Trauma and turmoil are not for you. If they come, you will deal with them, but you will never unnecessarily create or be a part of them.

You likely have a good imagination and are able to visualize things easily. You may have a rich dream life. You may also be highly perceptive, noticing details that others miss. You may be a good student.

You may have expanded intuitive and spiritual awareness and insight and may be able to perceive and influence the world of subtle energy. This might show up as hunches or just "knowing things" about people or events—all the way up to frequent and detailed psychic or clairvoyant experiences. You will have made the jump from ordinary to extraordinary reality.

Is Your Sixth Chakra Out Of Balance?

Someone with an underactive sixth chakra is likely to be out of touch with her or his intuition. You may be practical to a fault. You may try to solve all problems and answer all questions with logic or convention. Lacking intuition, you may belittle those who have it.

You are probably aware of experiencing only the material world—what you can see, hear, taste, touch or smell. Non-material realities will pass you by or make you very uncomfortable if you do experience them. Since they don't fit in your model of reality, you are likely to just ignore them.

You may miss details and nuances entirely, or on the other hand, you may be so mired in details that you miss the forest for the trees. You may see only what you want to see, think rigidly and view things in black-and-white ways.

You may feel like the world just doesn't make any sense, or you might be very simplistic in your interpretation of complex things. You may be cynical and negative.

You may have difficulty visualizing things that are not right in front of you. You may have limited imagination. You may not be able to remember your dreams.

You may be easily drawn into other peoples' problems, dwell on the negative and have lots of turmoil and drama in your own life.

As a child, you may have been laughed at for imaginary friends or an active imagination. If you had intuitions about things or experienced non-ordinary reality (as most children do, until they are taught not to), you may have been punished for talking about these experiences. You may have had unusual insight or precocious wisdom and been shamed for it as "getting too big for your britches."

Someone whose sixth chakra is overactive, on the other hand, may be overwhelmed by intuitive and psychic information, unable to process it or interpret it. You might be ungrounded and spacey, have your "head in the clouds" or even have delusions or hallucinations. Your imagination may run wild. You may be out of touch with others and have difficulty with the practicalities of life.

In either case, someone with an unbalanced sixth chakra may have visual or sensory problems (although poor eyesight alone is not a sign of an imbalance in the brow chakra). Headaches may be a problem for you. You may be plagued with nightmares or hallucinations.

Work With Your Sixth Chakra If...

In summary, it would benefit you to clear, balance and support growth in your sixth chakra if several of these statements apply to you:

- You'd like to think more clearly and be able to "see the big picture."
- You like to be more in touch with your intuition.
- You're seeking spiritual growth.
- You'd like to be more imaginative.
- You're interested in meditation, but haven't done it much yet.
- You live in an extremely logical culture.
- You live in an extremely materialist and materialistic culture.
- You'd like to have more vivid dreams or even just be able to remember your dreams.
- You're an extremely analytical, "just the facts" kind of person.
- You have difficulty concentrating.
- You're so busy that you rarely stop to reflect or just sit and observe.
- You watch a lot of TV.
- You feel like you're walking around in a fog.
- You pride yourself on being logical and scoff at those who are not.
- You often feel confused.
- Most issues seem very simple and black-and-white to you.
- As a child, you were laughed at or punished for seeing or experiencing things that others could not.
- You get so much intuitive or psychic information that it's overwhelming.
- You often gloss right over details.

- You're a little spacey and have a hard time relating to people and dealing with practical things.
- Your work is extremely intellectual or analytical.
- You have frequent headaches.
- You often miss the forest for the trees.
- You have frequent nightmares.
- You're interested in psychic phenomenon but believe you could never develop these abilities.
- You rarely or never have sudden insights or "just know" something.
- Being practical and hard-nosed is extremely important to you.
- It's hard for you to imagine something new or to visualize things that aren't right in front of you.
- You easily get tangled up in other people's problems and quarrels.
- You'd like to have more insight and wisdom.

How to Clear, Balance And Nurture Your Sixth Chakra

Here are some practical, down-to-earth things you can do to support sixth chakra health and radiance. Naturally, you don't have to do them all. Just choose the ones that sound enjoyable or useful to you. Once you see the pattern, you'll be able to think of your own, too. Remember, intention is the "secret ingredient."

Activities

- Listen for your intuition. Trust your non-logical mind. Ask the universe a question, then patiently wait and watch for the answer. Be prepared to wait from seconds to days and to have the answer come from within or without.
- Keep a dream journal.
- Create a vision board.
- Meditate, focusing your attention in the center of your head at the level of (or slightly above) the eyebrows.
- Draw or do another art form that requires close observation and concentration.
- Visualize each of the colors of the rainbow in turn.
- As much as possible, still your internal mental chatter.
- Look for patterns in your life.
- If your sixth chakra is underactive, let someone else take care of the practical things while you meditate, go on a retreat, read an inspiring book or just be intensely present. If your sixth is overactive, be sure you ground regularly. Focus on daily life: walk, cook, take care of animals and children, do ordinary things mindfully and with presence.

Physical Body

- Hold the acupressure point on your forehead, just between the eyebrows and up a little, for a minute each day.
- Imagine your head as a balloon. Allow it to float to an upright position, positioning your ears directly over your shoulders. Do this often to train yourself to maintain good spinal alignment.
- Close your eyes. Systematically relax all the external muscles around your eyes. Then soften the internal eye muscles, feeling the relaxation penetrate deep into your head. Rest like this for a while. Notice any images that arise in your mind's eye.
- If you haven't had your eyes checked in a while, do so.
- Get a scalp and face massage.
- Belly breathe, following your breath and letting go of thoughts.

Home

- Turn off the TV. Institute a daily quiet time. Reduce visual clutter.
- Create a space dedicated to meditation in your home or garden.
- Bring in high-calibration art.
- Light candles. Say a prayer as you light them.
- Clean the windows and mirrors.
- Put a dream journal by your bed and record your dreams when you first awake.
- Feed your sixth chakra with beauty and harmony throughout your home and garden.

Family, Friends and Community

- Organize a discussion group focused on great ideas or books.
- Spend time with family and friends who bring out the best in you.
- Reconnect with an older relative who has always seemed wise.
- If you have kids, choose your battles. Take the long view. See the best in them, even when they don't see it in themselves.

- Share intuitions with family and friends. Honor and respect the intuitive wisdom of the ones you love and expect them to do the same for you.
- Form a dream discussion group or a meditation group.
- Refuse to be pulled into the quarrels of friends and family. Refuse to be drawn into gossip or talking badly about others. Be compassionate about the problems of friends and family without taking them on as your own.
- Practice seeing the best in others.
- If you have children, go out into nature. Sit or walk slowly and observe closely. Notice how, as you wait patiently, more and more reveals itself to you. If it appeals to you, record your thoughts in a nature journal or sketchbook or with a camera.

Food

Emphasize simple, vegetarian foods. If you eat meat, make sure that the animals were ethically raised and slaughtered. Avoid alcohol and other consciousness-altering substances. Eat foods that are good for the eyes and brain, such as fatty fish, blueberries, sweet potatoes, walnuts, whole grains, tomatoes, broccoli and pumpkin seeds. Explore herbs such as rosemary, gingko, and gotu kola.

Work and Career

- Instead of solving everything with logic, see if you can use other parts of your mind. Value your intuition. Make time for dreaming and visioning.
- Take part in long-range planning or vision-creating for your organization.
Step back and take a fresh look at a problem.
- Eliminate distractions and reduce interruptions so that you can concentrate better.

- Refuse to take part in office gossip or petty workplace quarrels.
- Take a vacation or go to a conference with the intention of gaining a new perspective.
- Seek a mentor. Be willing to be a mentor for younger colleagues.

Travel

- Visit mountaintops or anywhere with impressive vistas.
- Go to great libraries, universities, art museums or spiritual centers.
- Go to the zoo. Observe the behavior of both the human and non-human animals.
- Visit places known for the beautiful quality of their light.
- Explore a culture that views life very differently from yours.
- Spend time any place that feeds your eyes with beauty, sparks your imagination, gives you clarity and perspective or creates a sense of elevation and harmony in your mind.

Colors

Indigo (deep blue) is the color of the sixth chakra. Wear or decorate a room in this rich color. In particular, you might see if you can find glasses with dark blue frames, or bring indigo into a library or study. Allow the color to remind you of your intention to develop your third eye.

Scents

Rosemary enhances mental function. Basil is also valuable for mental clarity, while clary sage supports vision. Sandalwood can be an aid to meditation and spiritual awareness. Frankincense has long been considered a sacred herb that enhances psychic abilities and a connection to the divine. Sage has a long history of use as a spiritual purifier and clarifier. (See Appendix 4 for information about how to work with essential oils.)

Affirmations

(See Appendix 5 for tips on how to work with affirmations.)
Repeat affirmations such as:
- My mind is clear and agile.
- I have keen insight and intuition.
- I have an open mind.
- I see and understand the "big picture."
- My intellect is a powerful tool for good.
- I see beyond the surface, reaching deep understanding of people and situations.
- I have access to wisdom from sources beyond my individual self.
- I see beauty and goodness all around me.
- I am easily able to shift my consciousness
- I am open to experiencing non-ordinary reality. I am comfortable with the unknown.
- I am a source of clarity, insight and light for myself and those around me.
- My imagination is vivid and powerful.
- I live in the light.
- I embrace the wisdom within me.
- I am open to greater and greater spiritual awareness.

A Sixth Chakra Blessing

May your wisdom serve others. May your insight bring you new levels of spiritual awareness. May you understand your true nature. May you see clearly in every way.

CHAPTER 15

Seventh Chakra: The Crowning Glory

Cultivate Your Spirit And Rise Above The Worries And Confusion Of Daily Life

The crown chakra is the highest of the seven chakras. It is located at the top of the head (or just above) and projects upward.

The keywords of the seventh chakra are "transcendence" and "pure consciousness." It is often pictured as a lotus flower, opening to allow spiritual awakening. It governs spirituality, spiritual growth and relationship with the divine.

The seventh chakra is an avenue to higher states of consciousness. As we develop it, we become increasingly aware of consciousness itself—the eternal part of us that is beyond ego, thought, feeling and body. This brings more harmony and peace to our lives.

When fully developed, the crown chakra is said to confer unity consciousness—the beyond-mental understanding that separateness from anything, including God, is an illusion. The fully developed seventh chakra unifies us with the Divine Source, as well as everything else in the universe. This is said to be unimaginably blissful.

The more connected we are to our spiritual source, the more harmonious our life can be. Many nagging issues just drop away; answers to deep questions and problems seem nearby. We know our spiritual purpose and experience a sense of wonder. We feel unconditional love and radiate it back to others. We are truly liberated, and can live a life of great clarity, meaning and value.

It is associated with the colors white and purple and the elements of consciousness or thought.

Seventh Chakra At A Glance

Common English Name	Crown Chakra
Location	Top of head
Associations	Spiritual life and experience, deep self-knowledge, sense of oneness and unity, relationship with the divine, pure consciousness, transcendence
Related organs	Upper skull, cerebral cortex, central nervous system, pituitary gland
Related sense	None
Related color	White or violet
Related element	Thought, consciousness
Ideal level of functioning	Highly spiritual approach to life, advanced understanding of spiritual matters, sense of relationship with the divine, sense of meaning and purpose in life, sense of wonder, feeling of kinship/unity with all beings, pure consciousness, transcendence

Is Your Seventh Chakra Healthy?

Someone with a healthy, balanced crown chakra will usually consider himself or herself deeply spiritual, though not necessarily conventionally religious. You may spend regular time in prayer, meditation or other devotions.

You're just as likely to be a gardener as an acknowledged spiritual leader—maybe more so. Although you are at a high level of spiritual development, you will not seek or require wealth, fame, status or even acknowledgment of this. Your ego—what's left of it—just doesn't need to be fed by conventional forms of success and achievement.

However, you may find that people (and animals) spontaneously seek you out for the sense of peace and wellbeing that they feel in your presence, recognizing you on some level as a spiritual teacher.

Whether you have a worldly, otherworldly or just a simple life, whatever you do is done humbly, mindfully and conscientiously, but with a kind of benign detachment. This comes from a comfortable awareness that the things of this world are only transitory, and from knowing, as the spiritual teacher Pema Chödrön says, that "whatever is happening is the path to enlightenment."

You have a sense of the meaning and sacredness of all things and feel connected to a higher power or larger purpose. You often feel a sense of wonder. You may feel, as author Jan Phillips observes, that "we are inches from the face of God." You have compassion for all humankind and a sense of kinship with all beings. You may have glimpses of unity-consciousness and profound spiritual joy.

You will be able to move beyond your individual ego to a more universal state of consciousness. You may have mystical experiences and be able to perceive the subtle energy world, although you are beyond ego attachment to such gifts. You may often be filled with a sense of joy, peace and bliss.

You are mentally stable and fairly well grounded, and although you may be indifferent to many social conventions, you probably still maintain at least a few close relationships. Although you are deeply kind, you will be able to witness much of life's ordinary drama and turmoil with an attitude of compassionate amusement and will not be drawn into it.

You enjoy peaceful activities. You may eat simply and be vegetarian or you may love a good meal, but in either case, eating, as with most things you do, will be done mindfully.

Your physical body may come in any shape or form. You radiate an almost palpable sense of peace, good will and kindness.

Is Your Seventh Chakra Out Of Balance?

If your seventh chakra is out of balance, spirit and body are in a state of separation.

If your seventh chakra is underactive or blocked, you may feel cut off from spirituality and the sacred and be plagued by a sense of meaninglessness and apathy. This might lead you into despair or into vainly trying to fill the void with physical pleasure, drugs, material objects, work or achievements that perpetually feel hollow once attained. You may frequently get caught up in the churning and theatrics of life. You may excessively seek society's conventional rewards and symbols of status.

An underactive or blocked seventh chakra may cause you to be highly skeptical, cynical and even hostile to authentic spiritual people and experiences. You may be superficially and narrow-mindedly attached to a particular religion, professing that all others are wrong. You may misuse religious institutions for personal power and gain.

As a child, you may have been punished or shamed for being too dreamy or not practical enough. You may have been forced to attend religious services or profess religious beliefs that did not resonate with your authentic spiritual self. You may have experienced trauma at the hands of religious figures or may have felt abandoned by God.

Alternatively, if your crown chakra is overactive or open too wide in relation to your other chakras, you might be delusional or grandiose. You may be overwhelmed by spiritual experiences that are beyond your ability to integrate.

You may be very ungrounded and spacey, with difficulty finishing tasks and tracking things on a practical level. People might think that you have no common sense whatsoever, and might describe you as having your head in the clouds. As a child, you may have experienced traumatic experiences that led you to disassociate from every-day life and seek solace in more abstract realms.

With regard to your physical body, if your seventh chakra is out of balance you may have problems with your brain, with cognition or brain chemistry imbalances such as depression, or with nervous system disorders.

Work With Your Seventh Chakra If...

In summary, it would benefit you to clear, balance and support growth in your seventh chakra if several of these statements apply to you:

- You want to rise above the worries and confusion of daily life and have a greater sense of peace, harmony and love.
- You have your head in the clouds so often that you often forget things or lose track of where you are going.
- You're currently questioning the religious or spiritual beliefs that you've held for a long time.
- Your personal library contains lots of books about personal and spiritual growth.
- As a child, you were traumatized by religious figures or in a religious setting.
- Your life feels empty and hollow.
- You have a lot of trouble being silent and still.
- You'd like a richer spiritual life.
- You often feel spacey, dazed or confused.
- You are over the age of 60.
- You feel angry with God.
- Someone close to you has recently died.
- You'd like deeper self-knowledge.
- You are having strange paranormal experiences and they make you uncomfortable.
- You are very attached to material things.
- You're afraid of dying.
- You have a lot of anger about conventional religion.
- You're questioning the meaning of life and why you're here.

- You feel extremely isolated.
- You are extremely ill, dying or have had a recent near-death experience.
- As a child, you felt abandoned by God.
- You've been thinking about starting a practice of regular meditation or prayer.
- You are highly skeptical of or cynical about anything having to do with religion, spirituality or non-ordinary experiences.
- You were very dreamy as a child and have worked hard to overcome it.
- You sometimes feel competitive with others about which of you is the most spiritually advanced.
- You are depressed or have had a history of depression.
- You've been wondering about what happens after death or before birth.
- You have been thinking a lot about the nature of time and space.
- You are a scientist or a religious figure.
- You have a nervous system disorder, Parkinson's or Alzheimer's.

How to Clear, Balance And Nurture Your Seventh Chakra

Here are some practical, "real-world" things you can do to support seventh chakra health and radiance. Of course, you don't have to do them all, and feel free to make up your own. And remember, intention is the activating ingredient.

Activities

- Take an ordinary day and offer it in its entirety, "warts and all," to the Divine (or to the higher good of the planet if you aren't comfortable with the concept of a divine power).
- Meditate.
- Surrender a problem to your higher power. Be grateful for the help that comes.
- Focus your awareness on your breath. As you breathe in and out, be aware that you are mingling molecules of "you" with molecules of "not-you," the external atmosphere. With each breath, allow the distinction between "you" and what you consider to be outside of you to blur. What other examples of this (the mingling of you and not-you, inside and outside, self and other) can you think of?
- Spend an extended time in stillness and silence. Hold the intention to be aware of the witness part of you that is beyond feelings and thoughts—your consciousness.
- Sit with a natural object to which you feel an affinity, such as a tree or large rock. Practice feeling its personhood and your connection to it.
- Forgive and even embrace your human imperfections.
- Do anything that makes you feel peaceful and harmonious.

Physical Body

- Find the acupressure point on the top of your head where imaginary lines drawn directly up from the top of the ears intersect with the midline of your skull. With the other hand, find your third eye point, between your eyebrows and up just a bit. Hold these two points simultaneously for one minute or more.
- Walk. Practice seeing the beauty in everything.
- Find a swimming pool or calm body of water and float.
- Place your awareness on the space above your head for a few moments. Place your awareness on your physical head for a few moments. Place your awareness on the space below your feet for a few moments. Place your awareness on your physical feet for a few moments.
- Close your eyes. Without looking, feel your hands. Maintain awareness of your hands for a minute or so.
- Think about the sun going down (or coming up). Is the sun really going down (or coming up)? Is your felt sense of the solar system stuck in the earth-centered worldview that Copernicus refuted in 1543? That's true for most of us! It can be a wonderful consciousness-opening and -flexing exercise to update that mistaken sense of the universe, not just mentally, but in your physical body.
- Set aside time every day to belly breathe, being conscious of each breath. (See Appendix 3 for instructions.) Feel the goodness of each breath. Feel how the universe supports your life with each breath.

Home

- Practice "calendar therapy." Cut back on your activities and establish blocks of free time to meditate, pray and just be.
- Create an altar or meditation space or just a space where you can be alone.

- Take a holiday from your plugged-in, over-stimulated life. Turn off the TV, your computer and your phone. How does that feel? What happens next?
- If you live in a noisy place, consider moving someplace quieter. If you can't do that, learn, as in meditation, to allow external noises to take you deeper into your stillness.
- Light a white candle. Watch the flame. Where does the light end?
- Be mindful, present and un-rushed in doing the activities of your daily life.
- As with the sixth chakra, nourish your crown chakra by creating beauty, harmony and serenity throughout your home and garden.

Family, Friends and Community

- If you are not part of a spiritual community, consider finding one that suits you, or join a meditation or prayer group. (If you prefer a solitary spiritual life, that's OK too, of course.)
- Find a spiritual friend, someone to whom you can communicate deeply about your spiritual life.
- Send healing energy to any place in your community that needs it.
- If you don't have a pet, get one or offer to pet-sit for a friend.
- Explain to extroverted friends that you need time alone.
- Stay in touch with the everyday lives of those you care about, but also practice letting other people's problems be their own.
- Practice seeing the beauty and goodness in everyone you encounter.

Food

As with the sixth chakra, consider switching to a simpler, more vegetarian diet, or at least eating animals that have been ethically raised and slaughtered. Eat mindfully. Avoid harmful, consciousness-altering substances such as alcohol, stimulants and other drugs.

Work and Career

- Practice doing what you do with a sense of non-attachment to outcomes, even as you do the best job possible.
- Whatever the exact nature of the work you do, aim to be a force for healing and elevating the energy of every situation and person you encounter.
- While still doing what is required by your job, change your point of view, regarding what you do as an offering to the sacred or divine, rather than simply earning a paycheck or being in service to an individual boss or organization.
- Be a uniting influence.
- Whenever the opportunity presents itself, help bring coworkers' awareness back to the highest meaning and purpose of the work you're doing together.
- Practice an attitude of namaste: "the divine in me bows to the divine in you."
- In any way possible, bring beauty, harmony and peace into your workplace and work relations.

Travel

- As with the sixth chakra, visit places such as mountaintops that offer high, clear vistas. From the "space between thoughts," dissolve separation and allow yourself to be a part of what you see.
- Go to places without light pollution, where at night you can see the stars in all their glory, or where you can see the Aurora Borealis.
- Visit sacred places, either human-made or natural.
- Find places in your own community that feel sacred or uplifting. Leave a small offering of gratitude.
- Spend time anywhere in nature. Be still.

Colors

Purple/violet and white are the colors of the seventh chakra. Wear clothing or decorate a room in white or a shade of purple that is pleasing to you, from pale lavender to deepest royal purple. Adding purple to a meditation room or an altar would be especially fitting. Allow it to remind you of your intention to balance and develop your crown chakra.

Scents

Breathe the seventh chakra scents of rose or lotus, either in the form of high quality essential oils, or the real flowers themselves. (See Appendix 4 for more information on how to use essential oils.) Feel the molecules mingling with yours as you breathe them in.

Affirmations

(See Appendix 5 for tips on how to work with affirmations.)
Repeat affirmations such as:
- I am connected to and supported by everything in the universe.
- I walk in complete peace and harmony.
- I embrace my own imperfections with love.
- My life, just as it is right now, is the perfect jumping-off-place for my next stage of evolution.
- I acknowledge the divine presence in myself as in each being.
- I dwell in the present. I am whole in each moment.
- I am open to experiencing my true nature.
- I am nourished and supported with each breath.
- I know my purpose for being on this planet and take joy in walking my unique path.
- I let go of worldly attachments and desires with ease and joy.
- I am able to let worries and concerns drift away as I sense the unconditional love and support all around me.

- I find my true nature in the space between thoughts.
- I find magnificence, beauty and wonder everywhere I look.
- I know that death is just the next phase of my being.
- I am one with everything I perceive.

A Seventh Chakra Blessing

May you be at peace. May you understand your true nature. May you understand that you are free. May you feel your inseparable connection to all that is, was and will be.

CHAPTER 16

Your Seven Chakras: A Holistic System

Your chakras function as a system, a whole, just like the organs of your body.

You don't want any of your chakras to be considerably out of balance with the others. As an example, while intellectual or intuitive brilliance might seem desirable, you wouldn't want to try to open your sixth chakra to an excessive degree in an attempt to attain intellectual or intuitive genius. This wouldn't be a positive thing—it would just put your energy system out of whack.

So we always work to bring our chakras into balance and alignment with the rest, rather than focusing heavily on developing any one chakra. Of course I'm not saying here that you shouldn't work with individual chakras that seem blocked, out of balance or ready to evolve to a new level. I'm just saying, don't overdo it with any one chakra.

You can't go wrong if you work with your chakras with the intention of bringing balance and wholeness to your life, rather than with the goal of becoming brilliant and remarkable in one particular area of your life.

Undue emphasis on an individual chakra is most likely to happen when someone is grasping for something in particular, rather than trying to bring his or her whole energy system toward greater health.

As an example from the world of spiritual growth and healing, some people, in an attempt to gain greater spiritual development, focus almost exclusively on developing the fourth, fifth, sixth and seventh chakras. They discount and ignore the first three chakras in a misguided attempt at spiritual evolution.

This just makes their energy top-heavy, while in their personal lives it's likely to make them spacey, ungrounded and ineffective. Meanwhile, the chakras (and the associated areas of their lives) that they ignore are likely to rear up and bite them while they aren't paying attention. Like our bodies, our energy systems will always attempt to restore balance.

So remember that you are looking for a balanced chakra system.

- The first chakra is the foundation for everything else. It provides structure and a sense of security—absolutely crucial—so don't ignore it or disdain it.
- The second chakra gives us the "flow" that we need to change, play, have joy and create.
- The third chakra plays a big role in physical health and in having the vitality and personal power we need to create the lives we were meant to live.
- The fourth chakra opens us to giving and receiving love and helps to connect us to everything else in the world.
- The fifth chakra helps us speak the truth, express our unique and wonderful selves, and fashion lives that express the fullness of who we are.
- The sixth chakra helps us think clearly, find wisdom, tap our intuition and move into extraordinary realms.

- The seventh chakra helps us to connect to our spiritual nature and to the Divine.

How could we possibly have a good, full life without any of those aspects?

In the next section, you'll learn three ways to balance and align your chakra system as a whole.

CHAPTER 17

Three Techniques For Balancing Your Chakra System As A Whole

These powerful but simple methods—two meditations and one hands-on technique—will help you balance your chakra system as a whole. I recommend that you do one of these exercises at least once a week. They will clear, balance, align and energize your body, mind and spirit.

Chakra Color Meditation 1

- Sit comfortably. Take some slow, deep breaths and allow your mind to slow down.
- Ground yourself, visualizing roots running from your first chakra or the soles of your feet deep into the earth. (See Appendix 1, How to Ground, for more detailed instructions.)
- Now visualize the following colors rising up one by one through your grounding roots:

1. Red (first chakra)
2. Orange (second chakra)
3. Yellow (third chakra)
4. Green (fourth chakra)
5. Light blue (fifth chakra)
6. Indigo (sixth chakra)
7. Violet (seventh chakra)

- Run each color individually up through your roots, through your body, to the top of your head, cascading out the top of your head and back to the ground. At the base of your neck, allow the color to stream down your arms, spilling out your fingers and back into the ground.
- Have the color flow be continuous. Allow red to transition smoothly to orange, the red flowing out of your head and hands while the orange flows into your feet and up your body, and so on with the other colors.
- Explore how each color feels in your body. Is it warm or cool? Thick or thin? What is its texture? How does it flow—with ease or with difficulty? Do any images pop into your head as you run each color? Any emotions?
- After you're done, take a few minutes to sit in silence and enjoy the feeling of balance and harmony.

Chakra Color Meditation 2

- Sit comfortably upright, feet flat on the floor and arms and hands relaxed. Take a few minutes to breathe deeply and slowly, all the way into the lower third of your lungs, so that your belly rises and falls as you inhale and exhale. Gently make your breathing slower and more regular.

- Direct your attention to your first chakra, located at the base of your spine. Visualize a wheel, spinning clockwise. Visualize or sense it as a pure red color. Breathe in red, breathe out red (either through your nose or through the first chakra). Allow the color red to permeate your body and your personal energy field. Stay lightly focused on the first chakra for a minute or so.
- Direct your attention to your second chakra, located in the middle of your lower abdomen, between your naval and the top of your pubic bone. Visualize it as a wheel of a pure, clean orange color, spinning clockwise. Breathe in orange, breathe out orange (once again, either through your nose or through the second chakra). Allow the color orange to permeate your body and your personal energy field. Stay lightly focused on the second chakra for a minute or so.
- Direct your attention to your third chakra, located in the middle of your upper abdomen, between your naval and the bottom of your sternum. Visualize it as a wheel of a pure, clean yellow color, spinning clockwise. Breathe in yellow, breathe out yellow. Allow the color yellow to permeate your body and your energy field. Stay lightly focused on the third chakra for a minute or so.
- Direct your attention to your fourth chakra. It is located in the center of your body at the heart level. Visualize it as a wheel of a pure, clean green color, spinning clockwise. Breathe in green, breathe out green. Allow the color green to permeate your body and your energy field. Stay lightly focused on the fourth chakra for a minute or so.
- Direct your attention to your fifth chakra, located at the base of your throat. Visualize it as a wheel of a pure, clean, sky blue color, spinning clockwise. Breathe in blue, breathe out blue. Allow the color blue to permeate your body and your energy field. Stay lightly focused on the fifth chakra for a minute or so.

- Direct your attention to your sixth chakra, located at the center of your forehead, between and slightly above your eyebrows. Visualize it as a wheel of a pure, clean, indigo color, spinning clockwise. Breathe in indigo, breathe out indigo. Allow indigo to permeate your body and your energy field. Stay lightly focused on the sixth chakra for a minute or so.
- Finally, direct your attention to your seventh chakra, located at the top of your head. Visualize it as a wheel of a pure, clean, violet (or white) color, spinning clockwise. Breathe in violet (or white), breathe out violet (or white). Allow the violet or white to permeate your body and your field. Stay lightly focused on your seventh chakra for a minute or so.

Now just relax and notice how you feel. Take a few moments to continue breathing in a slow, deep, relaxed way, just staying present to your body. When you feel ready to return from your chakra meditation, open your eyes and slowly return your attention to the room. You may want to ground yourself by drinking a glass of water, eating a piece of fruit or taking a walk.

Hands-On Chakra Balancer

This is a traditional, hands-on energy-healing method for chakra balancing. You can do it with your hands directly on your body in the area of each chakra, or a few inches above your body.

- Lie down in a comfortable place where you will not be disturbed.
- Spend some time breathing slowly and deeply. Take a few minutes to ground and center. (See Appendices 1 and 2 for instructions on how to do this.)

- Set an intention to balance and align your chakra system.
- Place one hand on your first chakra and one hand on your second chakra.
- Hold your hands in this position until you feel the energy equalize, you start to feel the energy pulse in a patterned way (e.g. in unison or regularly back and forth), or you get some other indication (such as just knowing) that the two chakras are balanced.
- Don't worry if you don't feel anything or don't get some other indication that the chakras are balanced. Just hold your hands on the two chakras for a minute or so, or until you feel that it's time to move on. Your intention to balance them will do the work.
- Move your hands to your second and third chakras and repeat the balancing.
- Move your hands to the third and fourth chakras and so on.
- After you've balanced the sixth and seventh, take a little while to enjoy the feeling. Being familiar with the feeling of having your chakras in balance will help you recreate the state whenever you want to.
- Get up and drink a glass of water. Enjoy the rest of your day.

CHAPTER 18

Some Final Thoughts

Differing Interpretations Of The 7 Chakras

If you go on to do more exploration about the chakras, you might find slightly different interpretations of each of the chakras than you have found here. That doesn't mean that any particular source is wrong. The truth is, most people, after they've seriously studied the chakras for a while, will develop slightly varying personal takes on what each chakra means. There will be lots of overlap, but details may vary. I think there's room for personal interpretation, and that it's healthy for people to come to their own conclusions.

My own interpretations are for the most part pretty mainstream, so they give you a good foundation from which to start. As you go on to experience the chakras on your own, I hope that you, too, will develop some of your own individual thoughts about their meaning, significance and associations.

In the meantime, the main thing is to enjoy your explorations of the chakras. I wish you self-knowledge, harmony, evolution—and fun!

APPENDIX 1

How To Ground

Grounding is one of the foundational skills of energy healing. It simply means connecting your energy to that of the earth. It's literally "being down to earth," in the best possible sense.

Grounding helps you orient yourself energetically to the earth instead of something external. This is important, because most external things aren't stable. The earth, by contrast, is stable, neutral and nourishing to your personal energy field.

Being grounded helps you feel more secure and balanced, lets you release excess energy to the earth and allows you to bring the earth's sustaining, steadying, healing energy into your personal field.

When you are solidly connected to the earth's energy, you can more easily be centered in your own body. You'll feel calmer, clearer, more present and more energized. You'll be harder to knock off your stride. You'll also be less likely to deplete your own energy, since you'll have access to the boundless energy of the earth.

There are many ways to ground, and when you get the hang of it you'll be able to do it just by touching the earth or even just by intending it. But in the meantime, here's a method you can use.

1. Sit somewhere comfortable, where you won't be disturbed. Sit with your spine straight.
2. Imagine roots extending down from your pelvis or the soles of your feet. Imagine them pressing into the earth and sinking deep into it.
3. Feel your connection to the earth. It's a strong, unshakeable connection. Sense the earth's energy.
4. Allow these roots to drain off any excess or unwanted energy in you—any tension, any fear or worry, any anger or bad feelings toward anyone or anything—into the earth, where it's neutralized.
5. Then allow the beautiful, calming, nourishing energy of the earth to be drawn up through your roots. Allow it to flow up through your legs, your pelvis, your torso, branching at your shoulders and running down your arms and into your hands. Allow the energy to continue up through your neck, into your head and your face.
6. Allow the earth's energy to feed your body and help you feel revitalized, refreshed and calm.
7. You can either contain the energy and circulate it through your body, or allow it to stream out your fingers and the top of your head and fall back down to the ground.
8. When you're ready, open your eyes and return to the here and now.

Appendix 2

How To Center

Centering is another foundational skill for energy work. It's simply focusing your energies and bringing yourself into the present. Another way of saying it is that it's centering your awareness in your own body.

Often our minds, emotions, and energies are all over the place. We're literally scattered. Our thoughts are on that weird thing the boss said at work yesterday, our hearts are with a loved one who's having trouble, and parts of our energy are stuck in the past, perhaps still traumatized by that year when we were four and our mother was too ill to take care of us properly.

Centering brings you—all of you—back to yourself, in the here and now. Being centered helps in doing most things, but especially in doing energy work. After all, if there's more of you present, you have more to work with.

Here's one way to do it.

1. Sit comfortably somewhere where you won't be disturbed. Sit tall.
2. Put your fingertips together with the fingers of the other hand, holding them lightly together in a position of comfort.
3. Breathe deeply.

4. As you breathe in, breathe in peace. As you breathe out, breathe out tension, worry and anything that doesn't serve you right now, at this exact moment.
5. Quiet your mind, letting go of thoughts.
6. Now, as you breathe in, imagine/feel that you are pulling the scattered parts of you back home to yourself with each breath.
7. Without thinking about it or trying, feel your energy being pulled back to you, back from all the places it has been scattered and fractured during the day.
8. With each breath, feel your energy becoming more whole. Feel it becoming more coherent. See or feel it coming back together, into wholeness, as if you are rewinding a movie of a pot or jar breaking
9. When you are ready, feel your energy, your essence, beginning to form a slight focus at the center of your chest, the center of your brow or anywhere else that feels natural and good.
10. When it feels right, open your eyes and come back to the present place and time.

Of course, there are many ways to center yourself. Just taking a few deep breaths can help. Meditation is also a powerful discipline for teaching yourself how to get and stay centered.

No matter how you do it, it feels great. Your breathing usually deepens and slows down, so that you're getting more oxygen in your system. You feel calm and stable. Your mind clears and your energy becomes more coherent and orderly. It's healing for body, mind and energy.

APPENDIX 3

How To Belly Breathe

Belly breathing is simple to learn and you can do it any time, anywhere, to relieve anxiety, stress and pain and improve mental clarity and long-term health.

It's also called diaphragmatic breathing, or sometimes just deep breathing. In its simplest form, it's just breathing fully so that the air reaches the lower third of your lungs.

It's the natural way to breathe when we're relaxed, but most Western adults don't do it. If you observe your own breath, you may note that you are breathing shallowly, into the top third of your lungs (chest breathing). If you are breathing more deeply, bringing the air more fully into your lungs, chances are you're still breathing shallowly and quickly. None of this is optimal, and among other things, it suggests that you are under stress.

Belly breathing works on a physiological level to help turn off your sympathetic nervous system (which produces "fight or flight" mode) and activate your parasympathetic nervous system (which produces "rest and digest" mode). This helps you relax—with profound benefits for your physical health as well as for your mental and emotional well-being. As simple as it is, it's one of the best things you can do for your overall wellness.

Here's how to belly breathe:

1. Inhaling through your nose, breathe all the way into the lower third of your lungs. Your belly should expand when you inhale and return to normal when you exhale. (Place your hands flat on your belly and watch them rise and fall to make sure that you're doing this correctly.) Breathing like this tells your body's stress mechanisms that danger is over and it's OK to relax. (It has a number of other wonderful health benefits, too.)
2. Breathe evenly, in a smooth rhythm. This relaxes you and helps you feel grounded. If it helps, you can count your breaths to help you keep the rhythm even. (As in "**IN** 1-2-3-4-5, **OUT** 1-2-3-4-5.")
3. After you've got the rhythm smooth and even, slow down the exhale in comparison to the inhale to super-charge the relaxation response. Aim to work up to exhaling about twice as long as you inhale. Long exhalations communicate with your nervous system, underscoring the message that it's OK to relax. Once again, if it helps, you can count to help you keep the proportion about right. (As in, "In 1-2-3-4-5-6, Out 1-2-3-4-5-6-7- 8-9-10-11-12," or whatever is comfortable for you. Keeping it comfortable is crucial—longer isn't better if it makes you uncomfortable.)
4. Breathe like this for at least a couple of minutes. Devoting at least five minutes a day to belly breathing is a great practice to maintain. It's also a good thing to do whenever you're feeling stressed, anxious, tired or like you're coming down with a cold.

Caution

If you start to feel dizzy or faint, just return to your normal breathing for a while. Because breathwork can make you light-headed, do not do breathing exercises while driving or operating heavy machinery (or standing on the edge of a cliff).

How Belly Breathing Benefits Your Subtle Energies

Your energy field when you're relaxed feels very different from when you're tense and anxious—smooth and flowing versus spiky and jagged. Breathwork, by helping you relax, helps your subtle energies shift more easily to a state of healthy balance and flow. It also helps you ground to your own body, connect your upper and lower chakras and unify the subtle and physical aspects of your being.

How Belly Breathing Benefits Your Physical Body

Among the most profound benefits of belly breathing are relaxation and stress reduction. Your body's "fight or flight" response to stress is necessary for survival when you're in dangerous circumstances or need to react to something quickly, but it has major health consequences if you get stuck in it—and most of us do.

Prolonged stress makes you vulnerable to illness and accelerates aging. Over time the stress response can contribute to high blood pressure, heart disease, ulcers, autoimmune diseases, cancer, anxiety, insomnia and depression.

Belly breathing, by allowing you to relax and relieve stress any time and anywhere, gives you a powerful tool for improving your physical health.

Appendix 4

How To Use Essential Oils

Essential oils are a beautiful way to support relaxation, balance and clear your subtle energies, manage stress and contribute to overall wellness. However, they can be powerful, and you do need to know a few things in order to work with them safely. Here are the basics.

What Essential Oils Are

Essential oils (EOs) are highly aromatic oils extracted from plants. Unlike artificially created perfume oils, they have healing properties, and unlike vegetable oils expressed from nuts and seeds, most of them are not actually oily. It takes a huge amount of plant material to make essential oils, and so some EOs can be wildly expensive. However, there are also many essential oils that are quite affordable.

EOs are highly concentrated, providing a powerful dose of natural therapy in a single drop. They have been used for healing, beauty treatment and body care for centuries.

I believe that essential oils, like homeopathy, work primarily on an energetic level—especially when they are used as a scent only, rather than applied directly to the skin.

Using Essential Oils

Essential oils can be used in a number of ways, however you should never ingest them (take them orally). The safest way to use them is simply to put a few drops on a tissue or cotton ball and inhale, taking care not to hold it too close to your nose. They can be very strong! If you <u>are</u> going to use them on your skin, you should always dilute them in a carrier oil—a maximum of five drops per ounce of oil. (They really go a long way.)

Carrier Oils

Carrier oils are used to dilute essential oils. Personally, I like jojoba oil best. Although it's a little pricey and can usually be found only at health food stores, it's great for the skin, absorbs quickly, has a neutral scent and never goes rancid. My next favorite carrier oil is grapeseed oil, a light oil that can usually be found at the grocery store.

You can spend a lot of money on carrier oils, but you can also use any food-grade oil in your cupboard. Just make sure that it hasn't gone rancid (it will have a bad smell), and for best effect, use an oil with a neutral odor.

Essential Oil Cautions

- Before using any new essential oil, read about its properties and cautions. They can be powerful, and not every oil is suitable for every person and every situation.
- Always keep EOs out of the reach of children. Do not use essential oils on children without discussing it first with their health care providers.

- If you are pregnant or nursing a baby or have heart disease, epilepsy, high blood pressure, diabetes or any other major health issue, seek the advice of a health care professional before using any aromatherapy/essential oils. They're powerful!
- Skin test all oils before using them topically. Apply a small amount of diluted oil (the equivalent of three to five drops essential oil to one ounce carrier oil) to the skin on your inner arm. Do not continue use if redness or irritation occurs.
- Do not ingest, either straight or blended. They are not intended to be taken orally.
- Keep all aromatherapy products away from your eyes and mucous membranes.
- If redness, burning, itching or irritation occurs, stop using the oil immediately. Wash the area with mild soap and water, dry, and then if it's practical, apply a little vegetable oil to the affected area, blot away as much as you can with a soft cloth and then wash with soap and water again. Consult your medical provider if self-treatment is not effective.
- Citrus oils are photosensitizers. Stay out of the sun after using them.
- Again, the safest way to use essential oils is simply as an environmental scent. Unless you know what you're doing, don't apply them to your skin.

Storing Essential Oils

EOs are volatile and will not last forever. You should cover them tightly after use and store them in a cool, dry place away from light.

APPENDIX 5

How To Use Affirmations

Here are some basic theories and instructions for working with affirmations.

What Is An Affirmation?

An affirmation is a positive statement of what you wish to be true, stated as if it is true. To your body-mind, it reads as true. Affirmations are a powerful method for using the mind-body connection to create positive realities for your body, mind and subtle energies. Some examples of affirmations are:

- My immune system is strong and effective.
- I am calm and centered in all circumstances.
- My heart and my life overflow with love.
- I am surrounded by amazing abundance.

The Theory Behind Affirmations

Science has proven the connection between mind, emotions and body. Our every thought and emotion causes a chemical response in our bodies. What we think and tell ourselves can either support or undermine our health and evolution. Positive thoughts and speech can help us make positive changes in our energy, bodies and lives. We can harness that amazing mind-body connection for wellbeing by using affirmations.

Guidelines For Creating Affirmations

- Keep them simple. Only address one issue at a time.
- Make them present tense. Say, "I have health," or "I am healthy," rather than "I will be healthy," or "I will have health."
- State things in a positive way. Avoid use of the word "not." For example, say, "I am well," rather than "I am not sick."
- Repeat them several times a day, either out loud or in writing, for about two minutes per session. Some experts say to repeat them for at least 30 days in a row to get the maximum effect.
- As you repeat them, try to stay strongly connected to your desire. (In other words, say it like you mean it!)

Glossary

Affirmation: An affirmation is a positive statement of what you wish to be true, stated as if it is true. To your body, it "reads" as true.

Belly breathing: Breathing for optimal health, all the way into the lower third of the lungs. When done properly, the belly will rise with the inhale and fall with the exhale. (See Appendix 3.)

Body-mind: The body, mind, emotions and energy regarded as a single indivisible unit, rather than as separate parts of a person.

Calibration: The quality of energy or vibration; adjusting the quality of energy or vibration.

Central channel: The energetic organ, running vertically up the center of the body, which is the equivalent of the physical spine. Energy runs up and down this channel.

Chakra: An energy center within the personal energy system, through which energy is exchanged with the universe. There are seven major chakras, located along the centerline of the upper body.

Clairvoyant: Having the ability to intuitively see events, people or objects in the future or non-locally, beyond normal sensory contact.

Energy: Life-force and being-force. Your energy—also called your energy field, energy system, energy body, spirit or chi—is what gives you life and being.

Energy field: The distinct and unique energy surrounding any particular being or thing.

Energy healer: A person who influences the energy of another person with the intention to heal their energy.

Essential oils: Highly aromatic oils extracted from plants. Unlike artificial fragrances, they have energetic and healing properties.

Intention: Using thoughts consciously and purposefully to create what is wanted.

Mandala: A geometric design, usually a circle, symbolic of the universe, used in Hinduism and Buddhism as an aid to meditation.

Unity consciousness: The beyond-mental understanding that separateness from anything, including God, is an illusion.

Further Resources

If you want more information about chakras, I highly recommend that you start with *Wheels of Life* or *The Sevenfold Journey*, both by chakra authority Anodea Judith.

- Judith, Anodea. Wheels of Life: A User's Guide to the Chakra System. St. Paul, MN: Llewellyn Publications, 2002. Print.
- Judith, Anodea, and Selene Vega. The Sevenfold Journey: Reclaiming Mind, Body & Spirit Through the Chakras. Freedom, CA: Crossing, 1993. Print.

For information about energy healing in general, some good resources are:

- Brennan, Barbara Ann. Hands of Light: A Guide to Healing Through the Human Energy Field: A New Paradigm for the Human Being in Health, Relationship, and Disease. Toronto: Bantam, 1988. Print.
- Eden, Donna, and David Feinstein. Energy Medicine. New York: Jeremy P. Tarcher/Putnam, 1999. Print.
- Hausauer, Nancy. The Energy Healing Site. Web. <http://www.The-Energy-Healing-Site.com/>.

Image Credits

Chapter 3: What Are Chakras?
Standing front image of chakras, adapted from image © Little_prince | Dreamstime.com
Side image of chakras, © 2013 Dane G. Meyer

Chapter 5: How Can I Tell If My Chakra System Is Healthy?
Side image of chakras, © 2013 Dane G. Meyer

Chapter Nine: First Chakra
Standing side view image of first chakra, © 2013 Dane G. Meyer

Chapter Ten: Second Chakra
Standing side view image of second chakra, © 2013 Dane G. Meyer

Chapter Eleven: Third Chakra
Standing side view image of third chakra, © 2013 Dane G. Meyer

Chapter Twelve: Fourth Chakra
Standing side view image of fourth chakra, © 2013 Dane G. Meyer

Chapter Thirteen: Fifth Chakra
Standing side view image of fifth chakra, © 2013 Dane G. Meyer

Chapter Fourteen: Sixth Chakra
Standing side view image of sixth chakra, © 2013 Dane G. Meyer

Chapter Fifteen: Seventh Chakra
Standing side view image of seventh chakra, © 2013 Dane G. Meyer

Back Cover
Nancy Hausauer by Dane G. Meyer, © 2013 Dane G. Meyer

Made in the USA
Charleston, SC
08 October 2014